Hawai'i's Pets

Photos of Our Animal 'Ohana

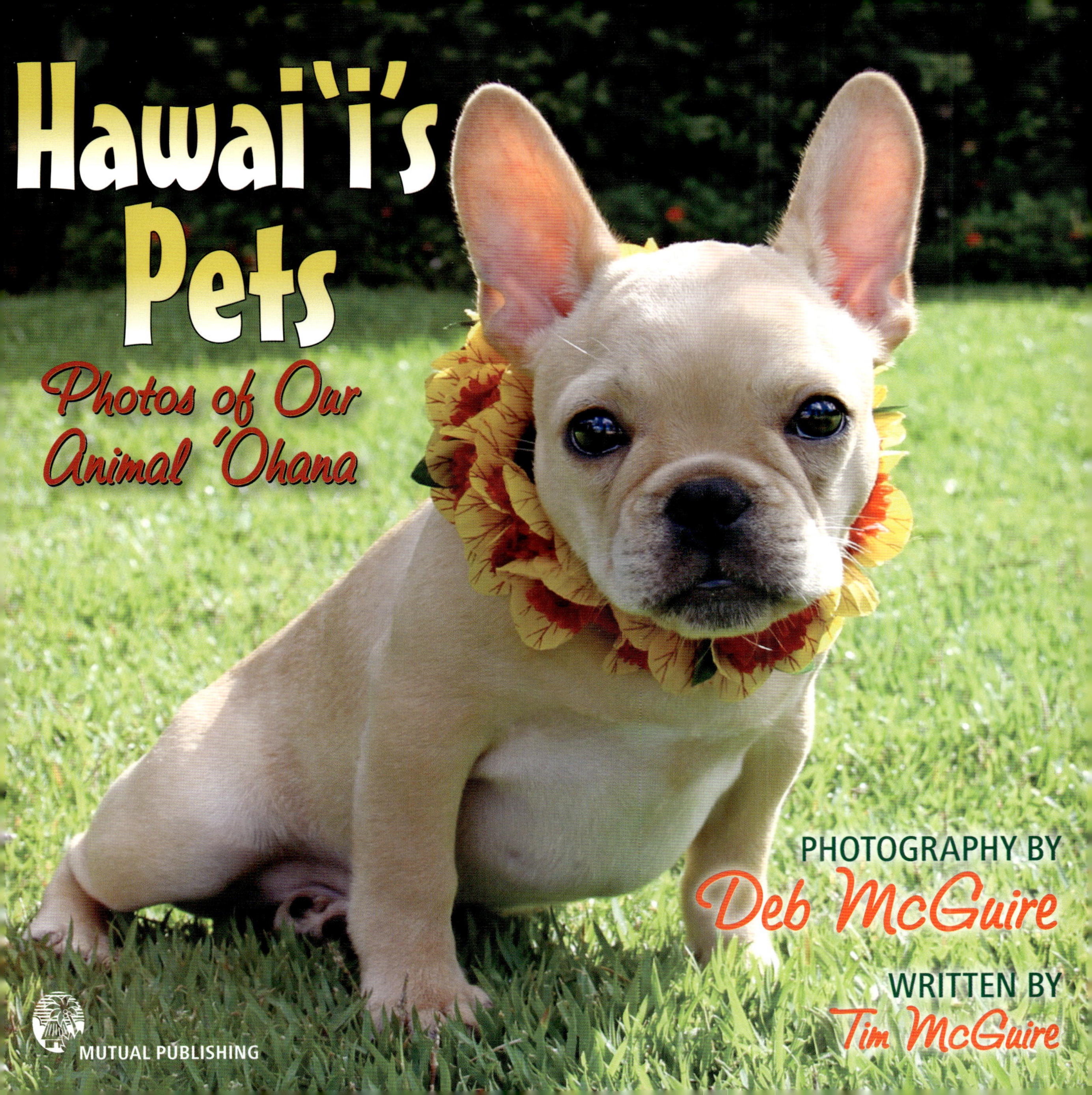

PHOTOGRAPHY BY
Deb McGuire

WRITTEN BY
Tim McGuire

MUTUAL PUBLISHING

Hawaiian Humane Society

People for animals. Animals for people.

For more than 100 years, Hawaiian Humane Society has championed the relationship between people and animals. We were formed on the grounds of ʻIolani Palace with King Kalākaua as a founding member. In our earliest days we strived to protect working animals, unwed mothers, and homeless children. Our mission to create a "humane society" has always been about people as much as animals.

Deb McGuire's *Hawaiʻi's Pets: Photos of Our Animal ʻOhana* is a beautiful, yet amusing book showcasing a variety of local pets in some of our islands' most scenic settings. No other book showcases the joy and love our animals have to offer us. We are pleased to be a part of Deb McGuire's first book, and hope you will enjoy the unique images she has captured as much as we have.

Mutual Publishing is donating a portion of the proceeds from this book to help the thousands of animals that Hawaiian Humane Society serves so proudly. As an independent and local nonprofit committed to helping kamaʻāina animals, we are grateful to Mutual Publishing and Deb McGuire for this donation. We hope you enjoy this book as much as we do.

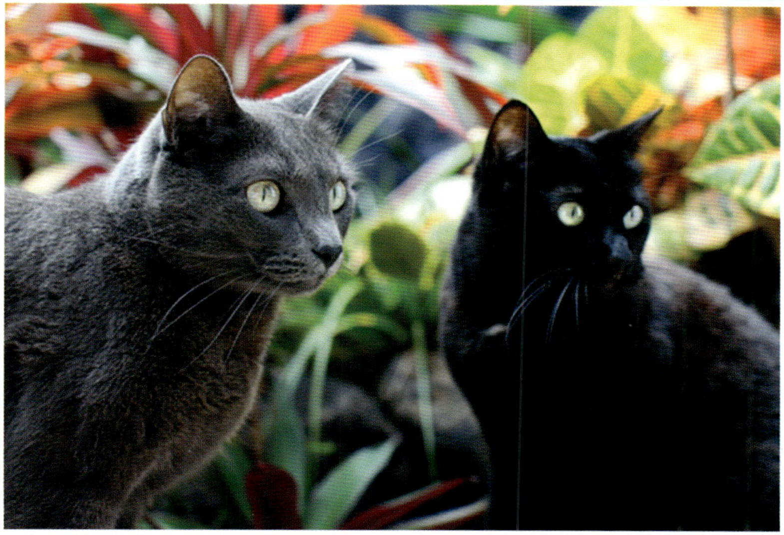

This book is dedicated to my cats, **Magic** and **Sham-rock**, for their many sacrifices and incredible patience, particularly when being chased through the house with a camera as I documented their every move.

It is also dedicated to by unbelievably supportive husband **Tim** who gets fired from Deb McGuire Pet Photography on a weekly basis but returns with a smile (or maybe it's a smirk) and is willing to work for little or no pay. He is my best friend, #1 fan and the one who makes me laugh the most in this world.

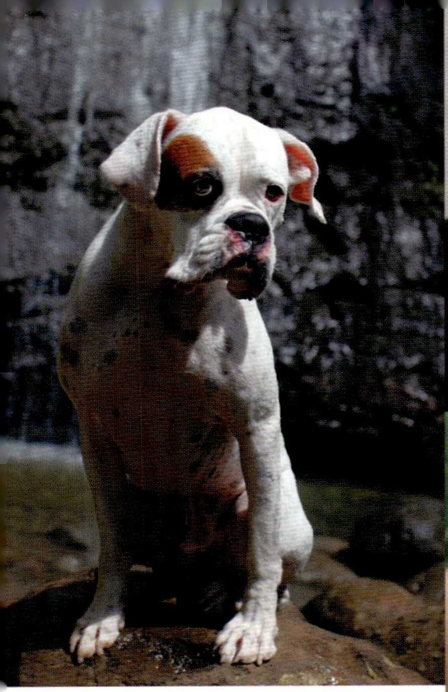
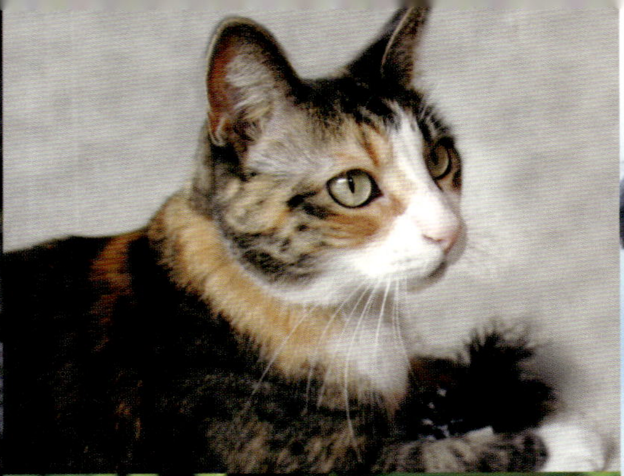
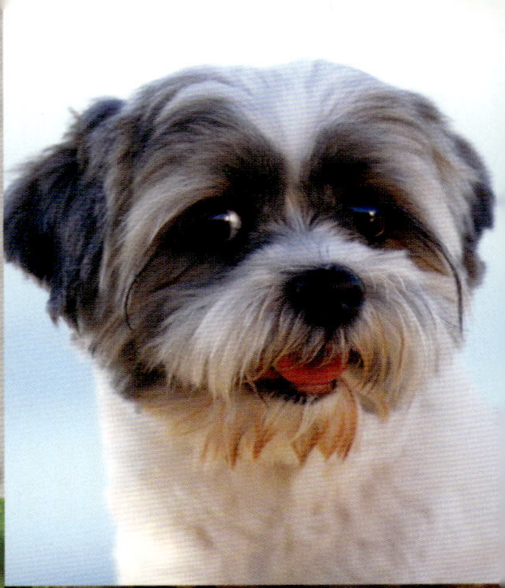
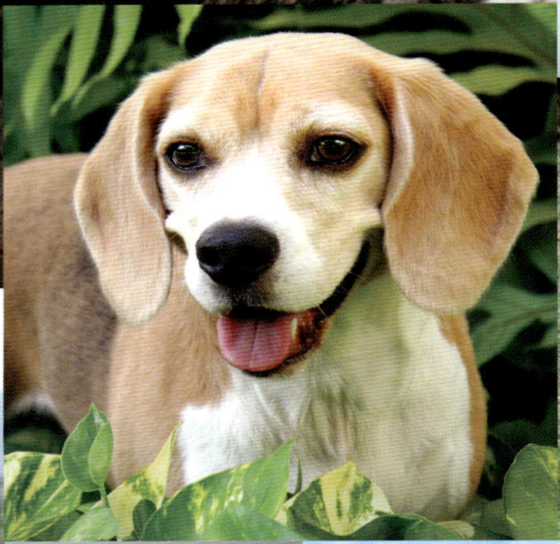
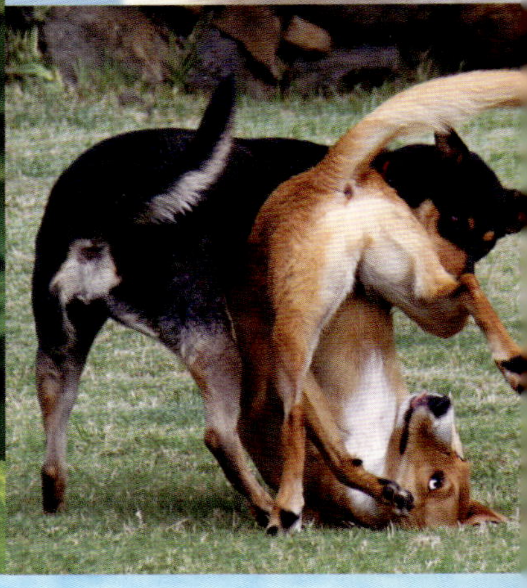
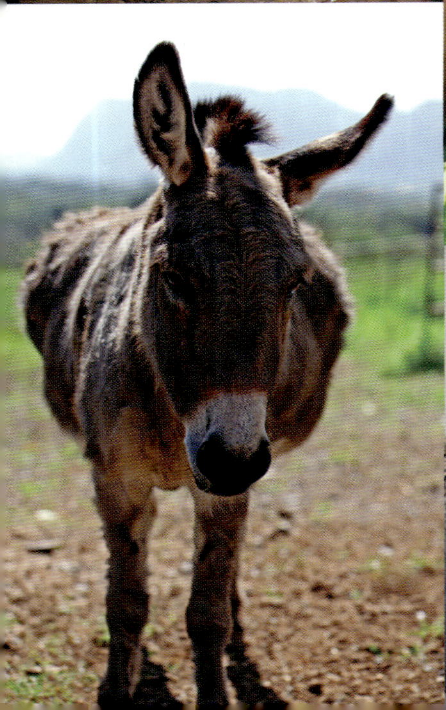
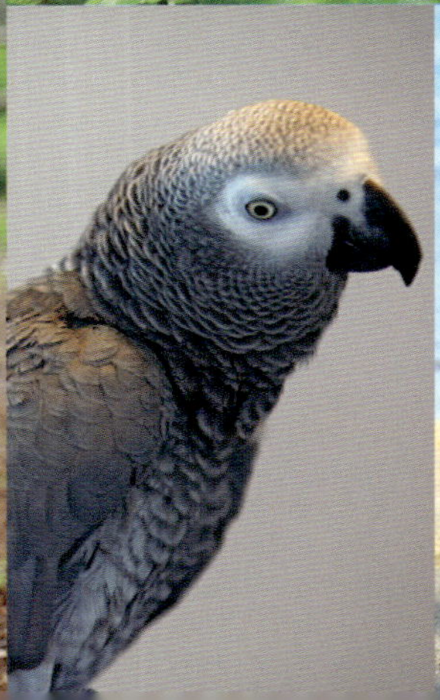
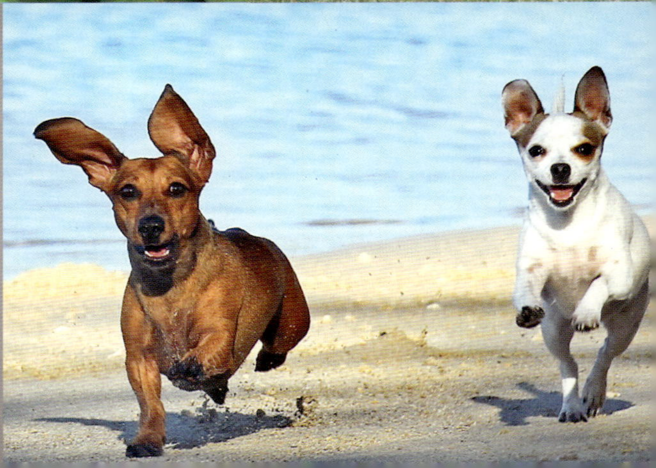

Why Pet Photography?
Why this book?

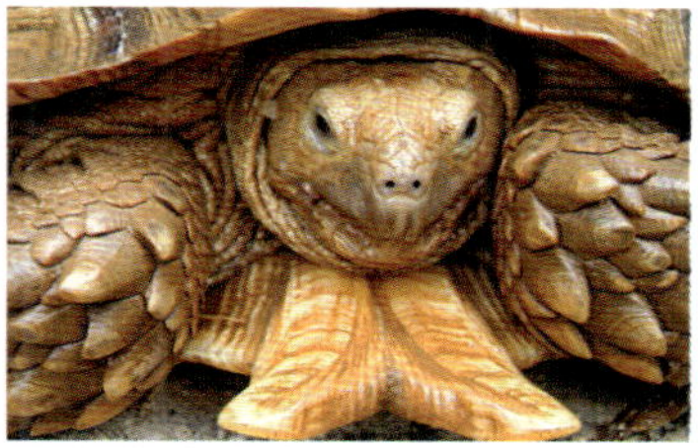

My life's passion is animals. Growing up the youngest of three girls, I have no memories of a home without pets. In high school, when I took my first photography class, my dog Heidi modeled; if she minded, Heidi did not show it. Through the years, several cameras, and a multitude of worldwide venues, I have focused my lens on furry and feathered creatures of all shapes and sizes. Whether it was an African safari or a hike in a South American rainforest or an overnight stay in a Thai jungle, I collected unbelievable photos that chronicled amazing animals in their habitats. At that point I began to seriously consider making my hobby a career.

Then, with my supportive husband at my side, I consulted with the most important members of our family, our cats, Magic and Shamrock. They understood and gave me their two-paws-up. They had only one request: be the best. Also, they insisted that the pets be the primary focus. Of course, I agreed, thus, the motto: "Animals are my passion, photographing them is my privilege."

I do nothing to make my furry friends feel uncomfortable. I photograph on location where the pets are most at ease. I go to their garden, their living rooms, a favorite park, the beach; the best place for pet photography is where the pets feel most comfortable. My photography is about the animals first; the photography comes second.

And now, I have reached a point that I want to share my joy, the images that I have captured. This collection chronicles Hawai'i's pets in some of the Hawaiian Islands' best scenery. I love all these furry and feathered friends that I have been so very blessed to photograph.

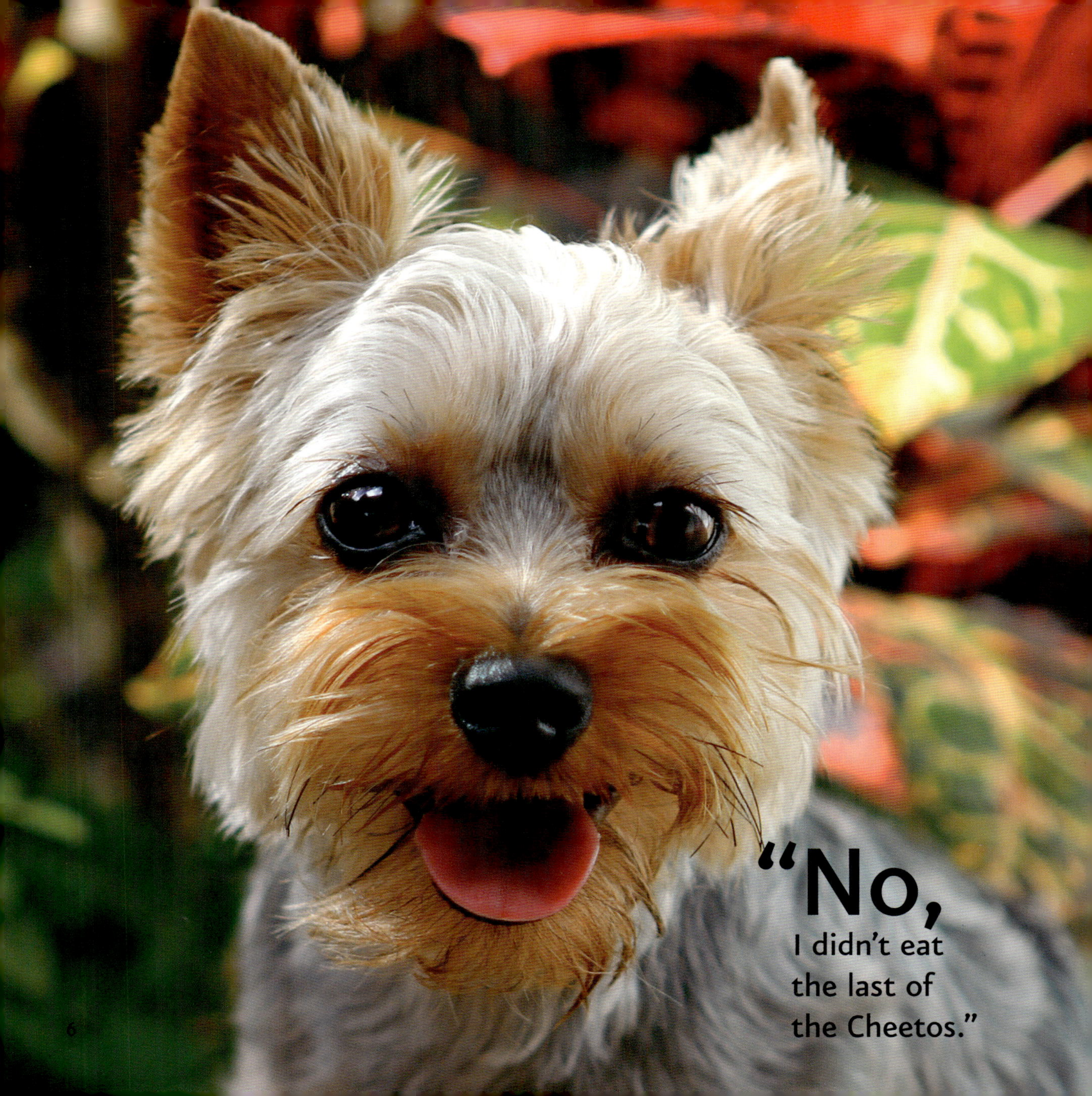

"No, I didn't eat the last of the Cheetos."

"Of course I drove.
It's called a
DRIVE THRU."

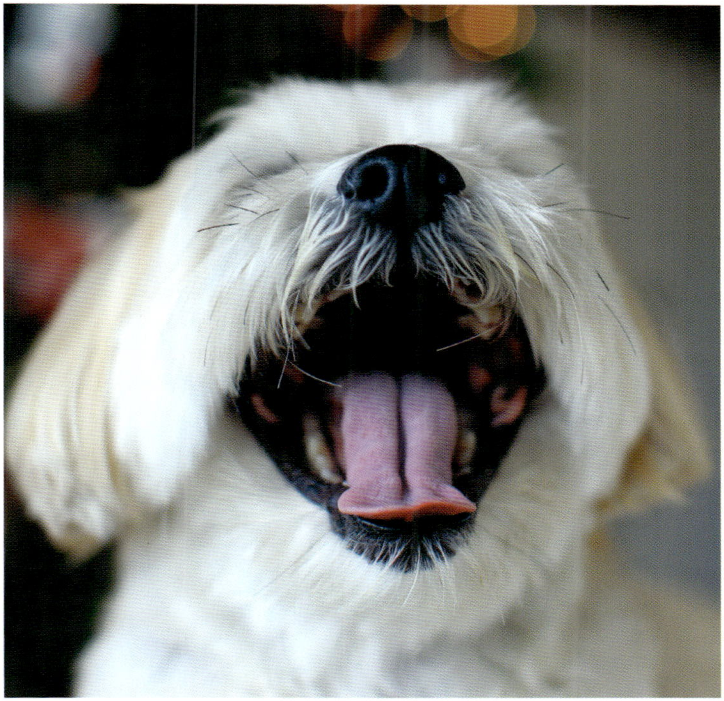

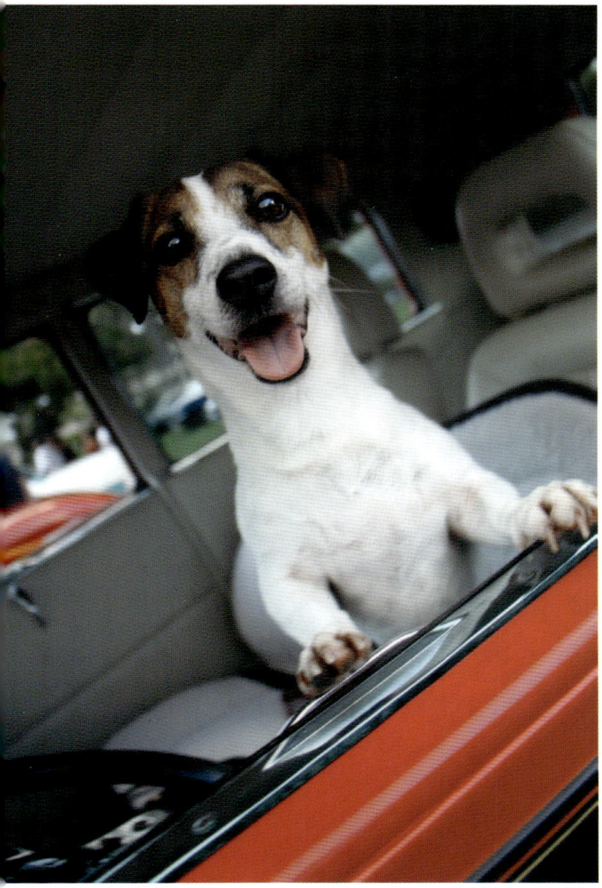

INSERT
DOG
TREAT
HERE

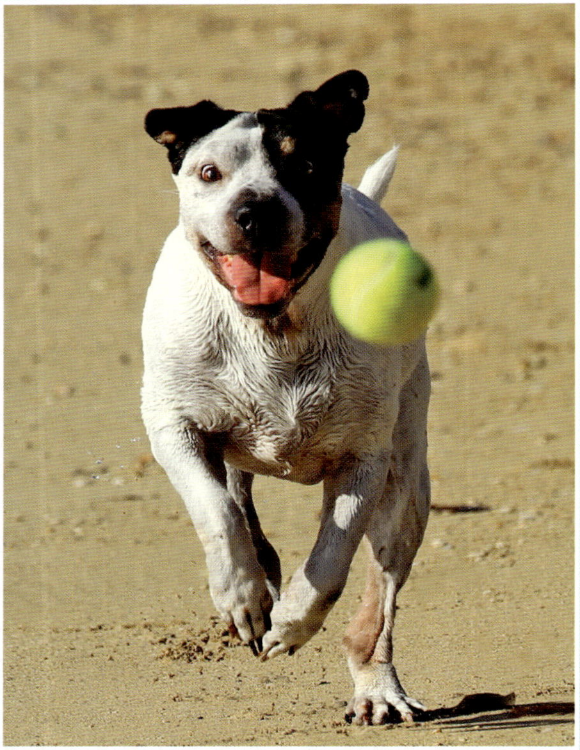

If dogs could vote on the world's greatest invention, the **TENNIS BALL** would be high on their list.

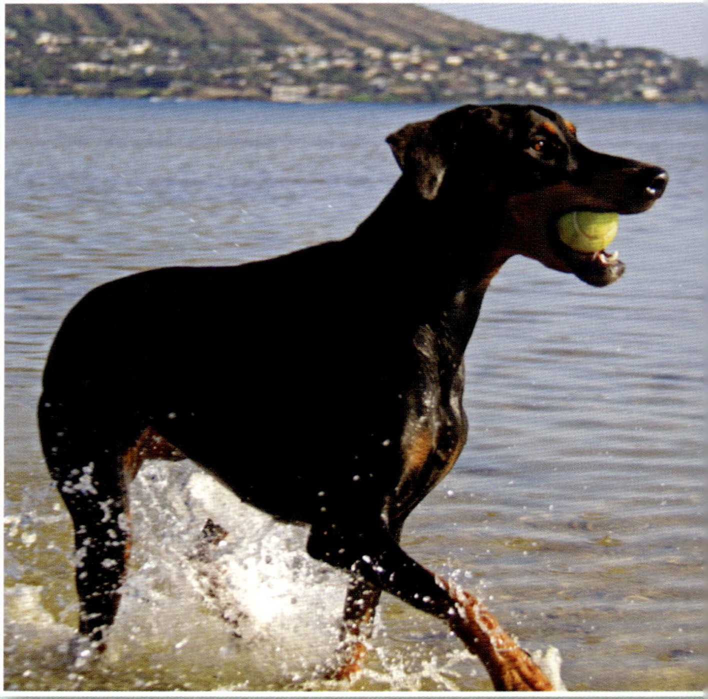

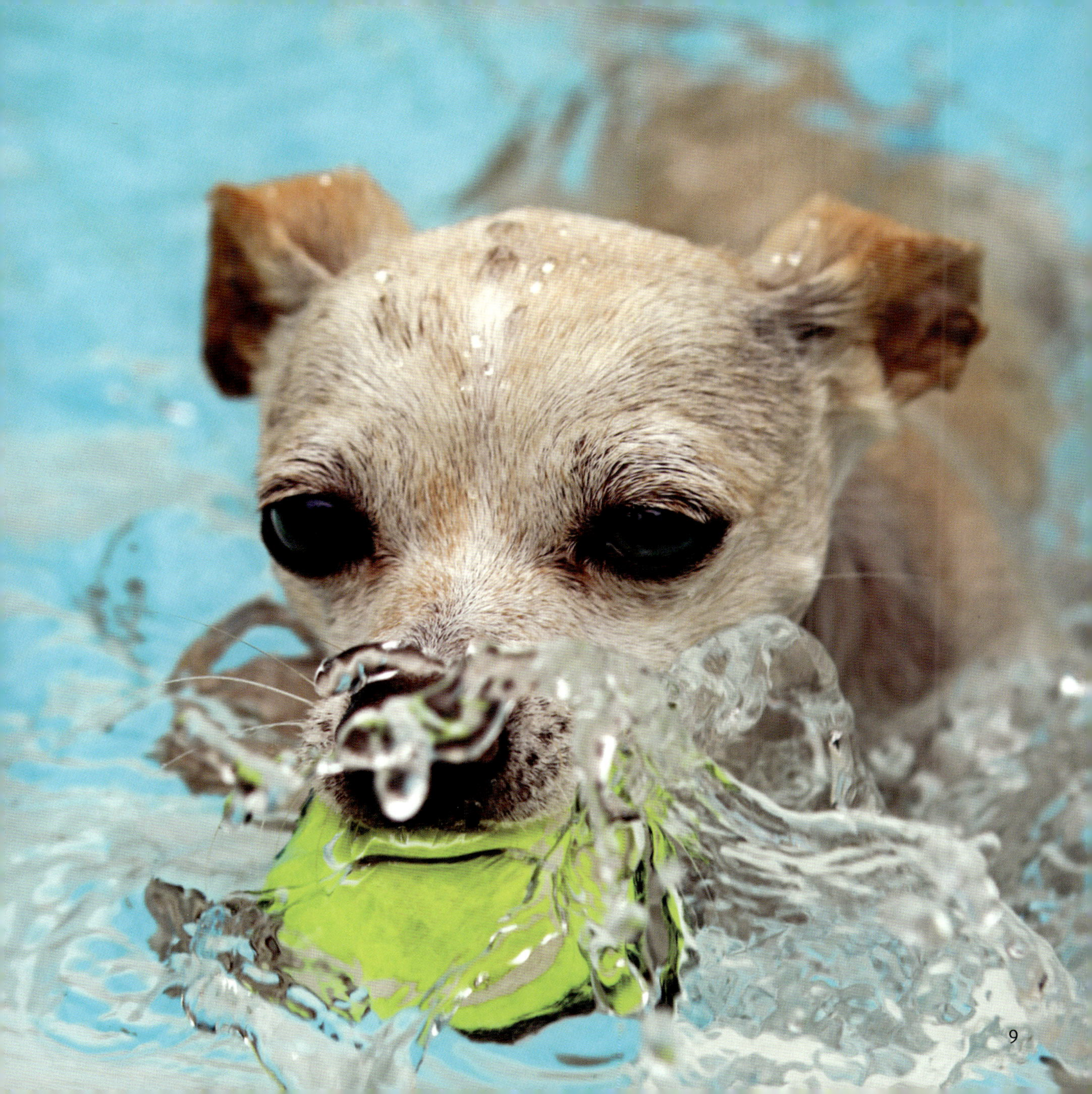

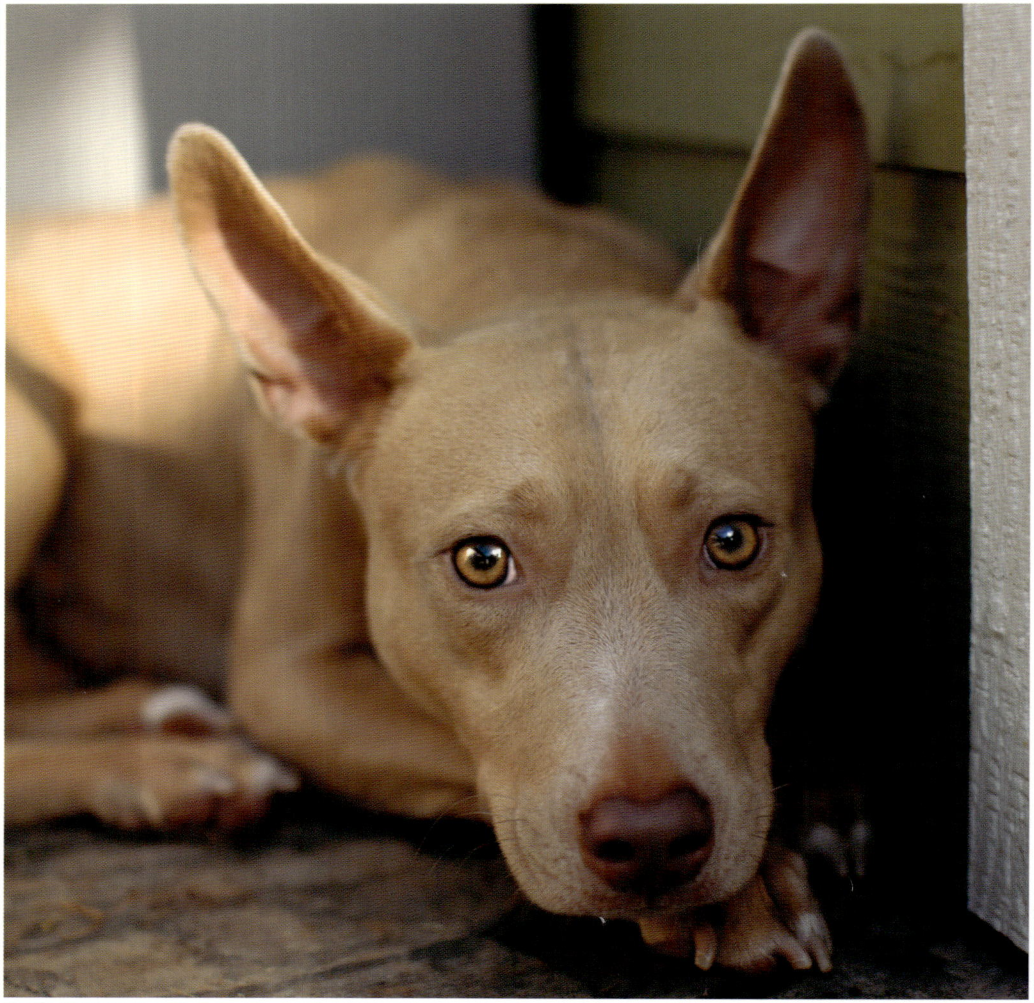

"Being a model is **SO DEMORALIZING.** I spent hours in front of a mirror perfecting this look. He just sits there and **WOWS** everyone!"

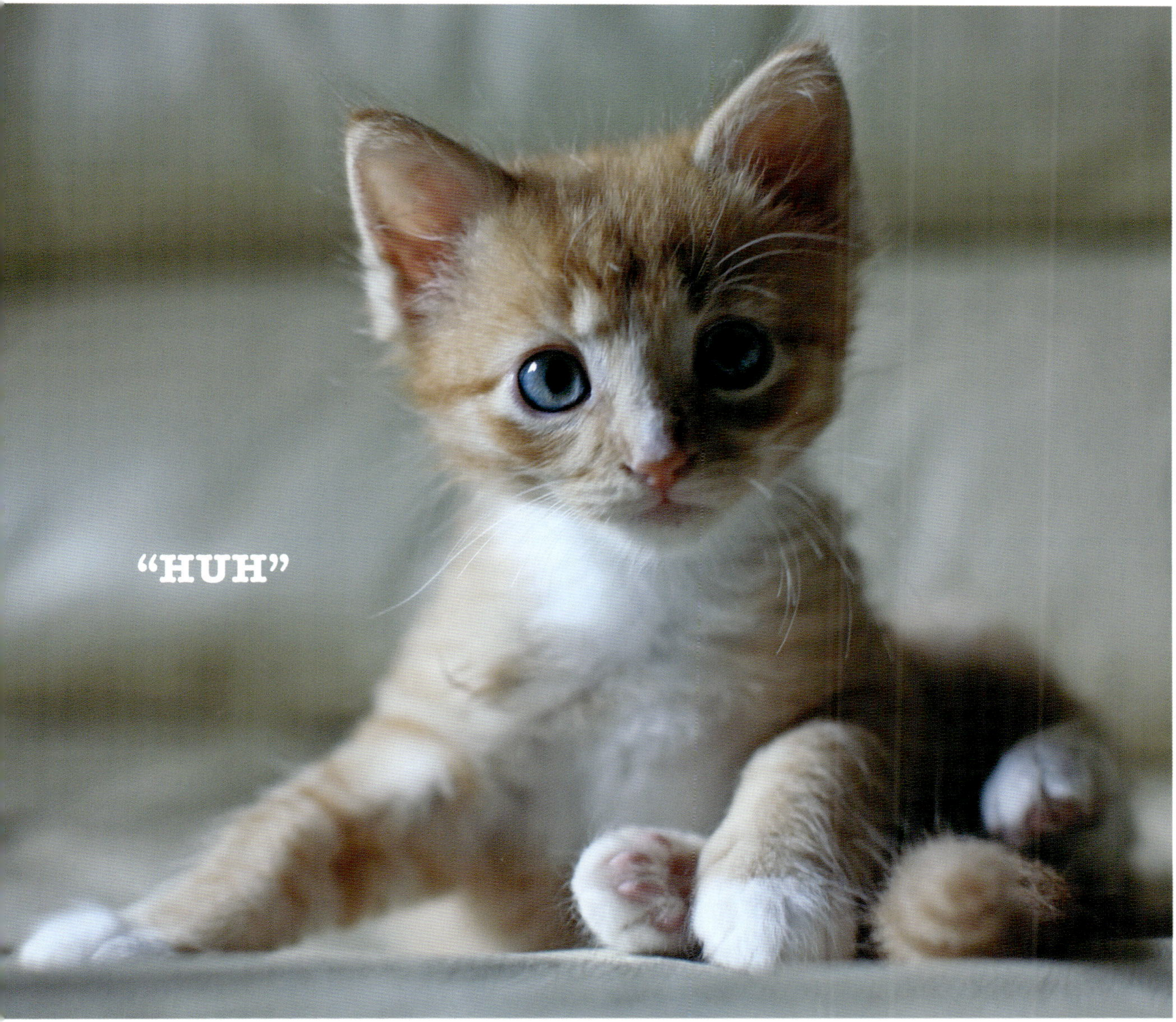

Tip: Focus on the eyes.

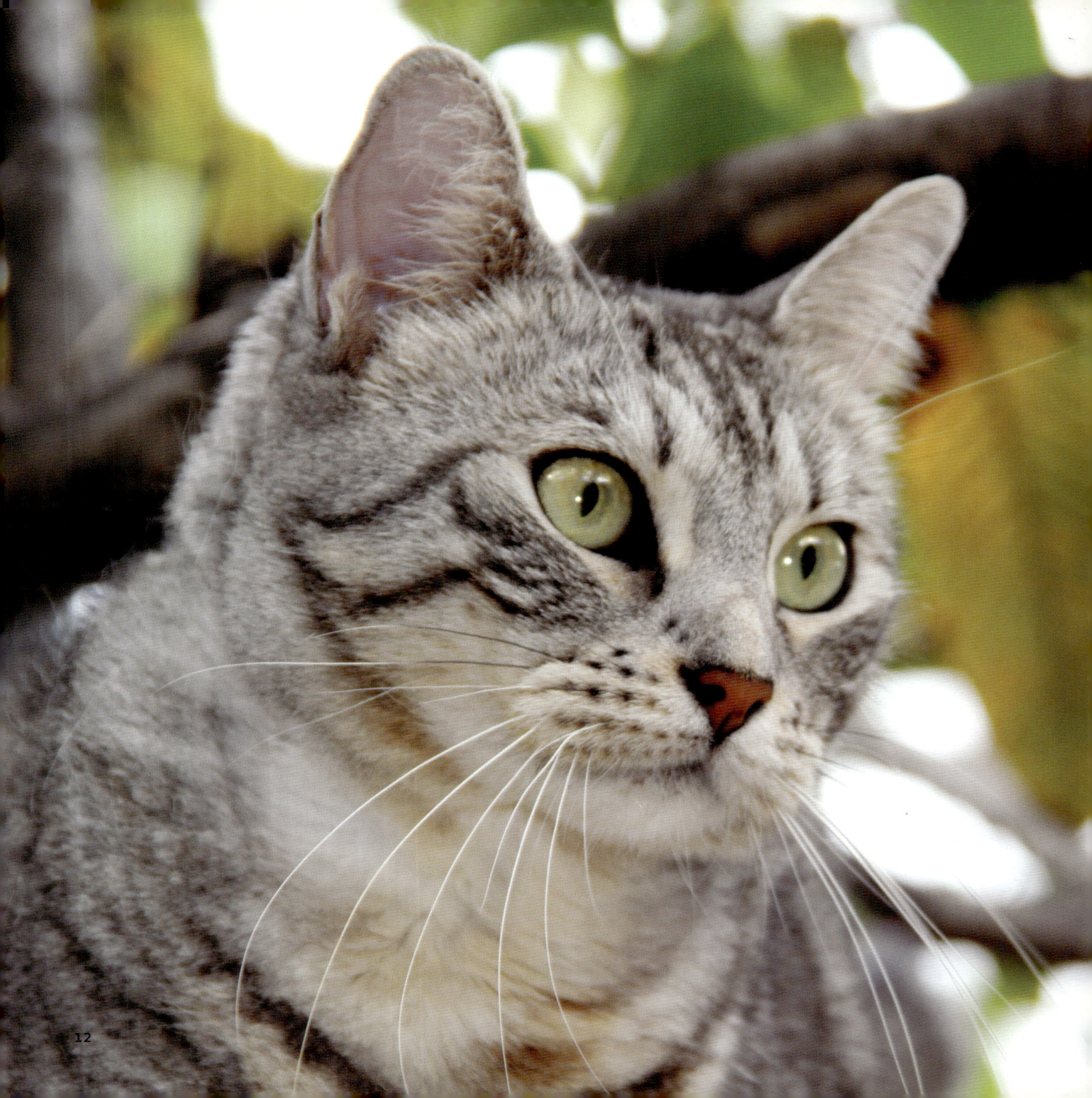

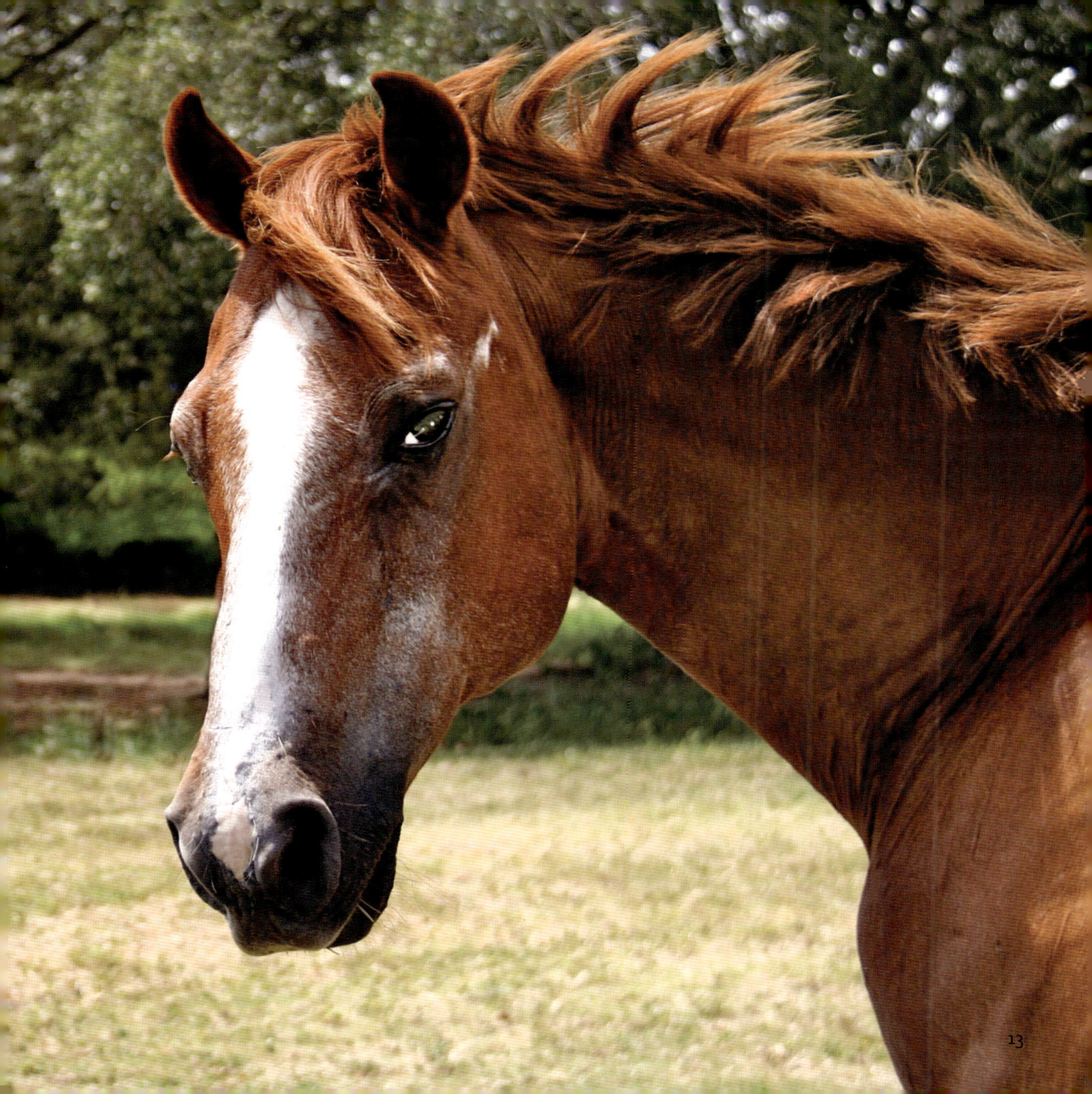

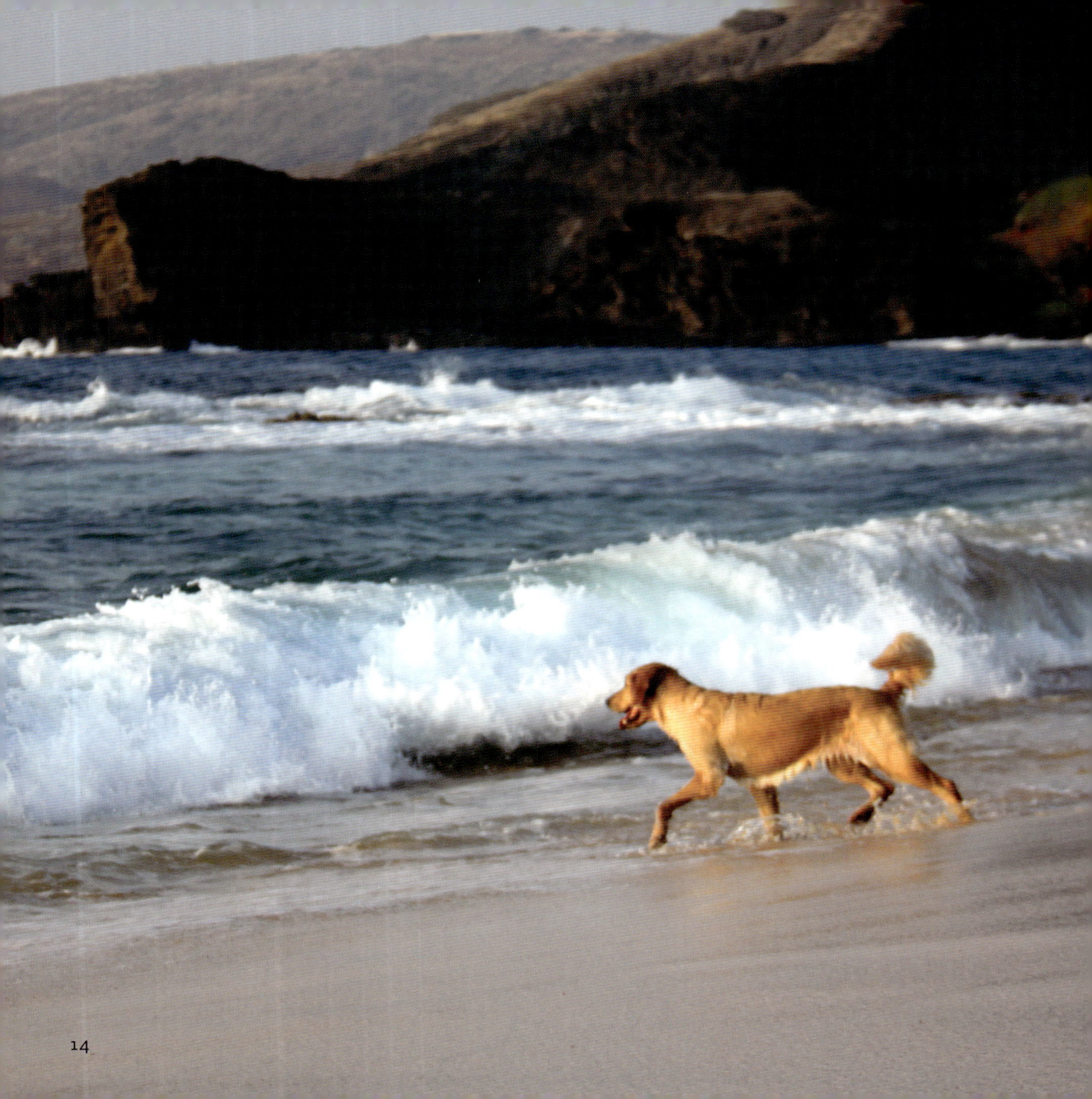

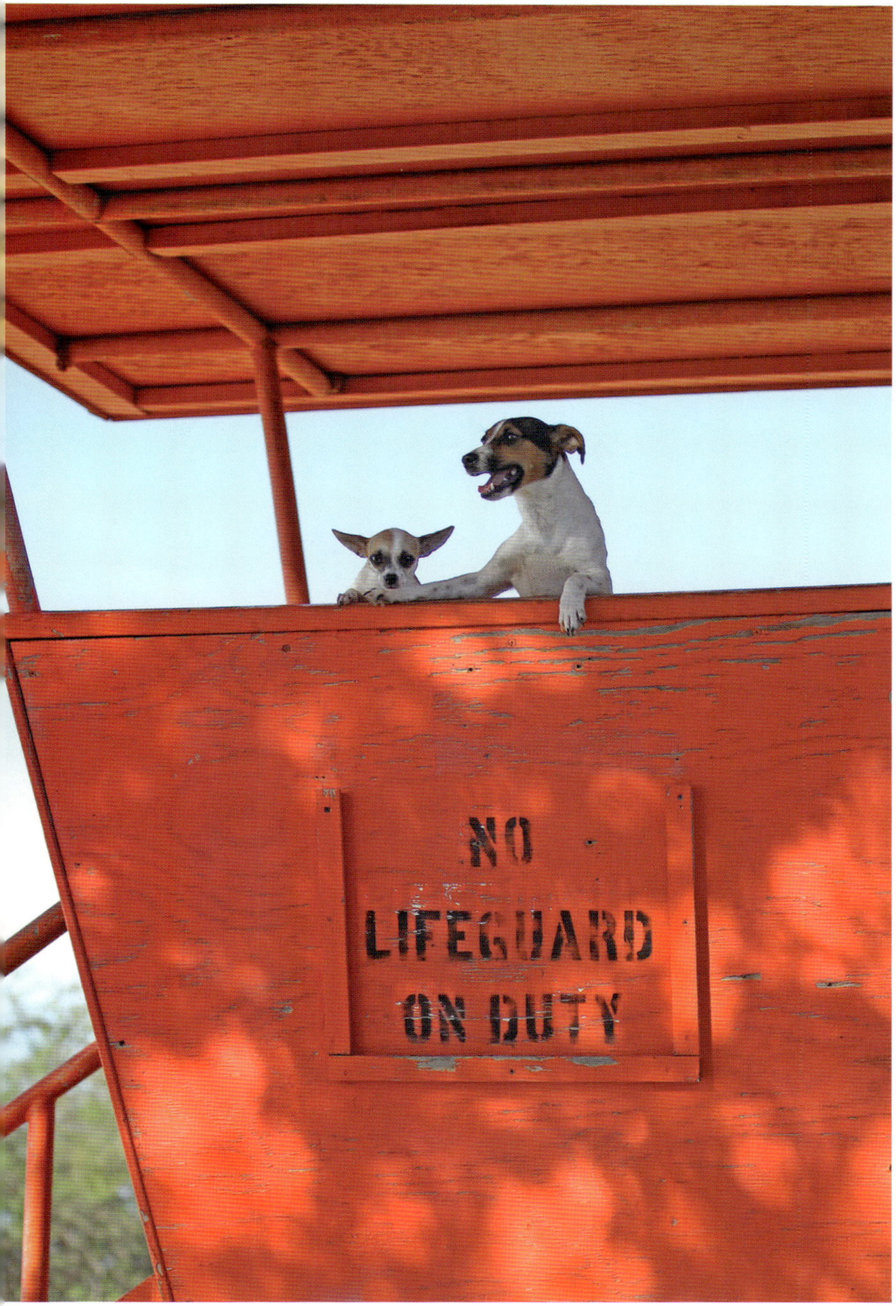

"'NO LIFEGUARD ON DUTY?!'
We're here!
Everybody in
the water!"

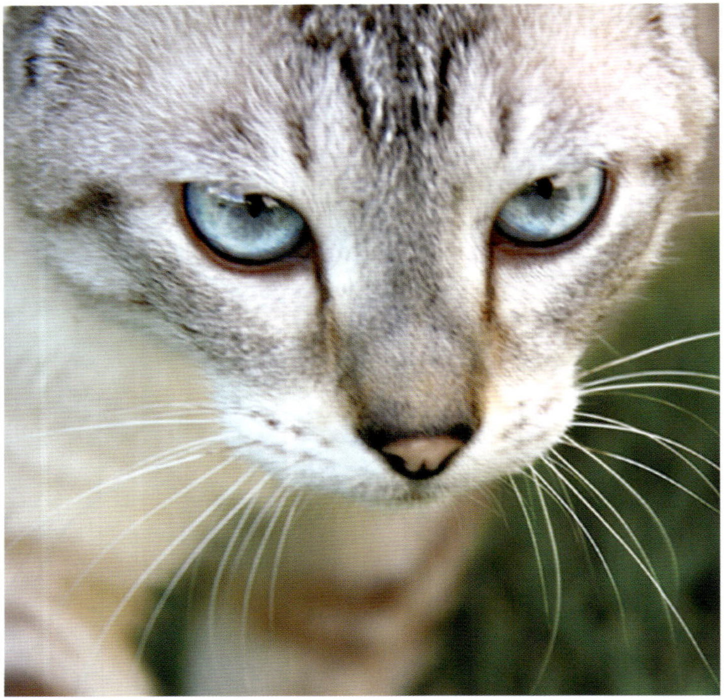

"These eyes
are talking to you.
Look deeply into them.
No, No!
Not too close, you just may
FALL IN LOVE."

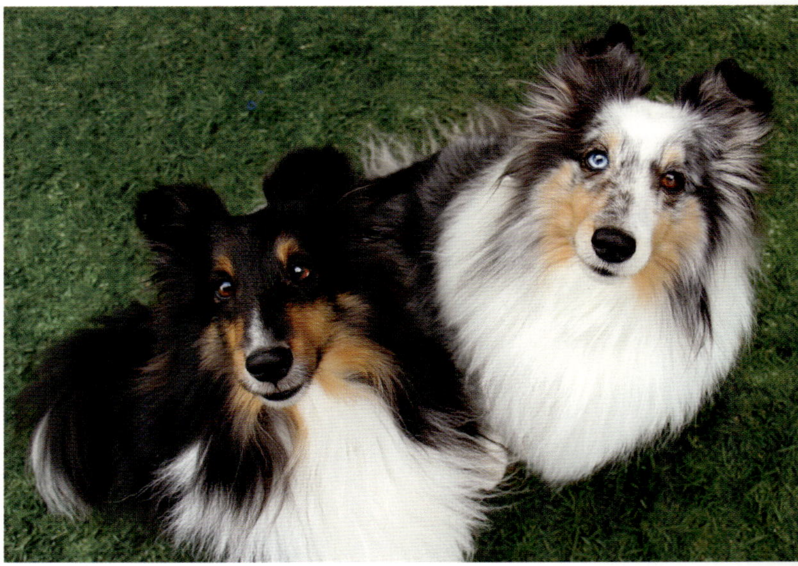

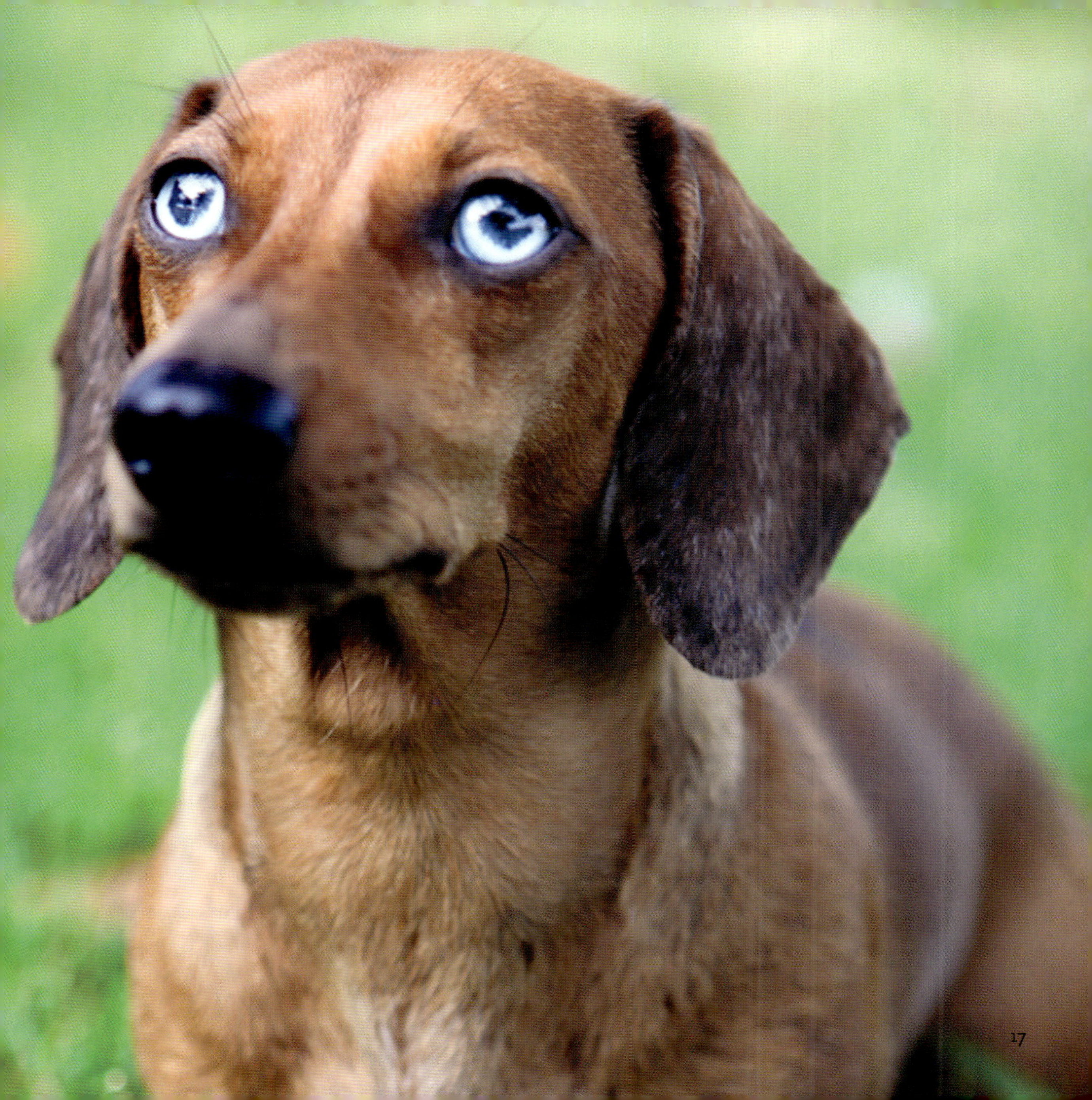

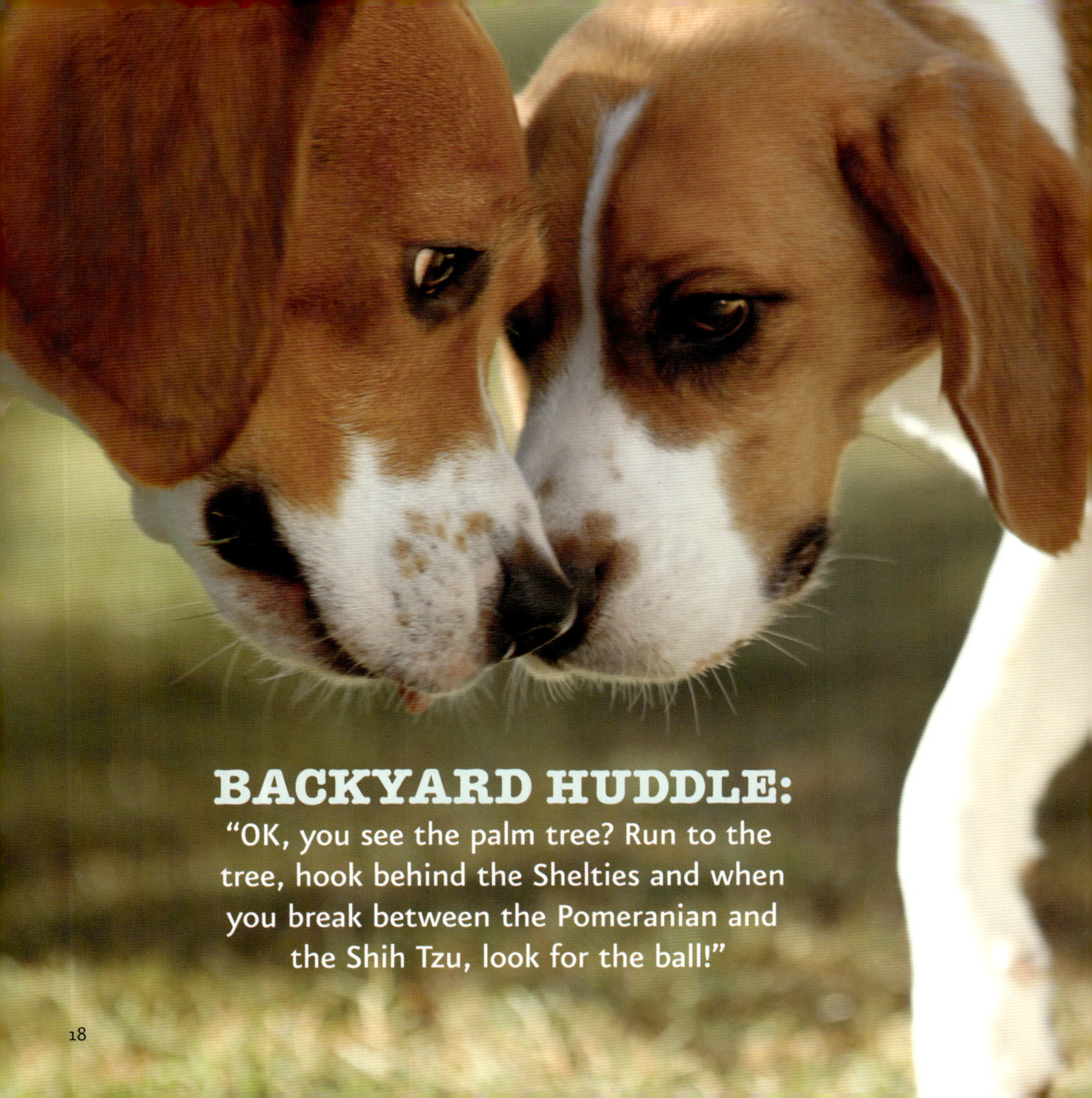

BACKYARD HUDDLE:

"OK, you see the palm tree? Run to the tree, hook behind the Shelties and when you break between the Pomeranian and the Shih Tzu, look for the ball!"

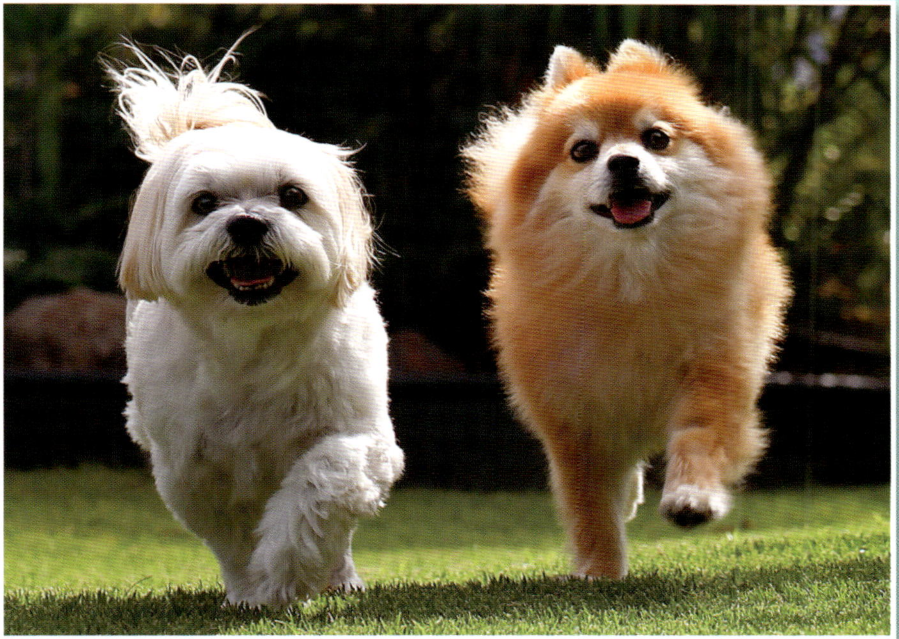

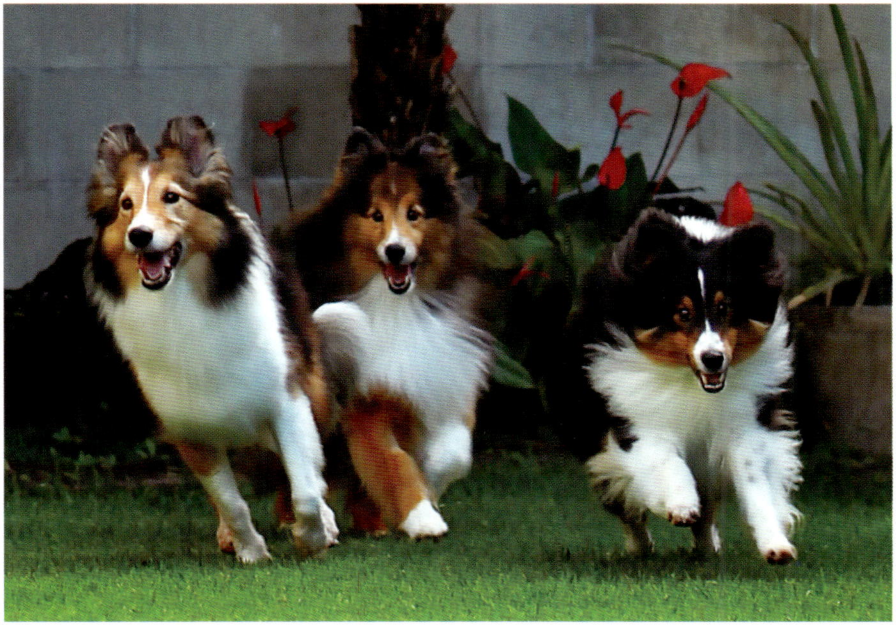

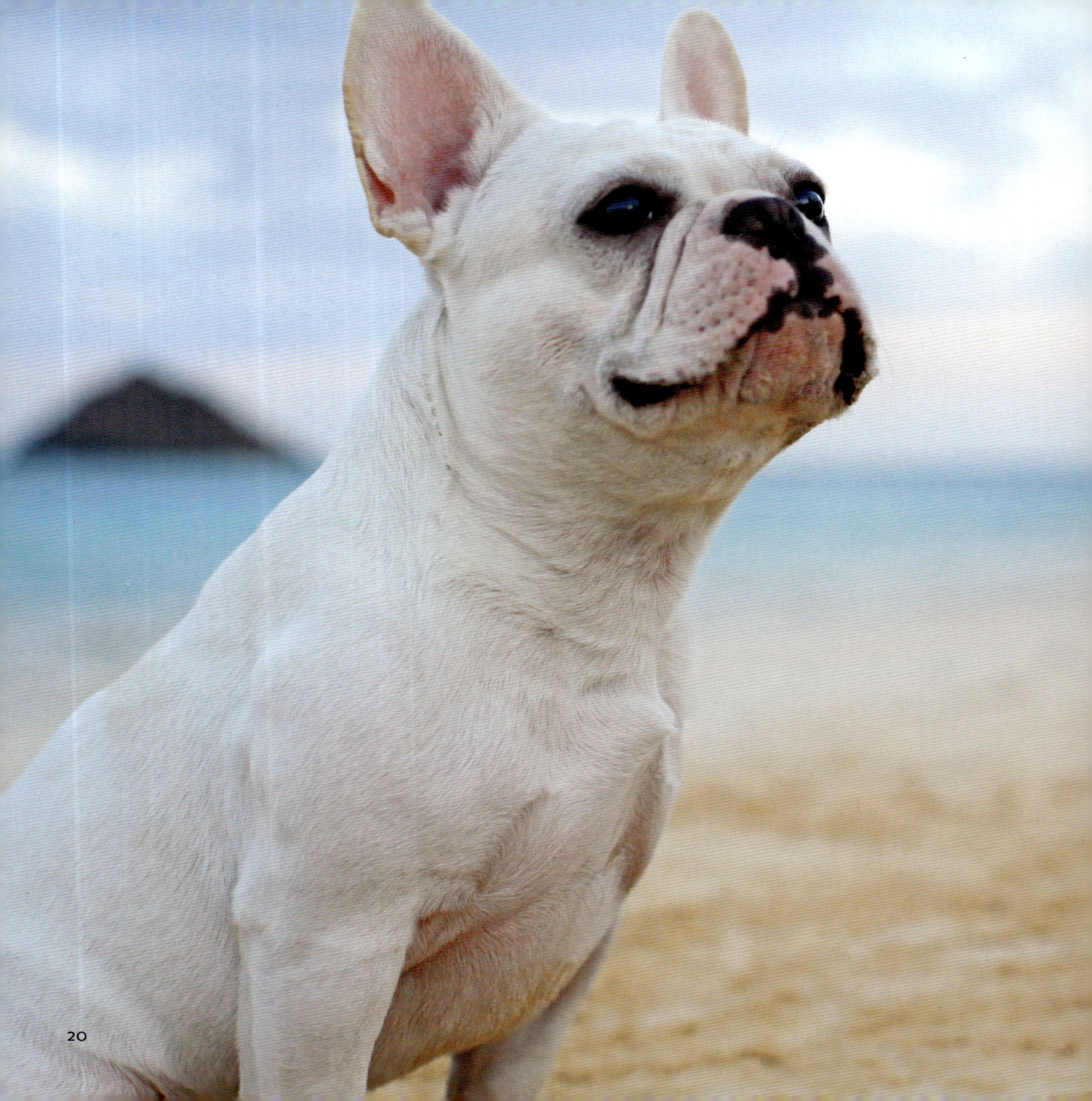

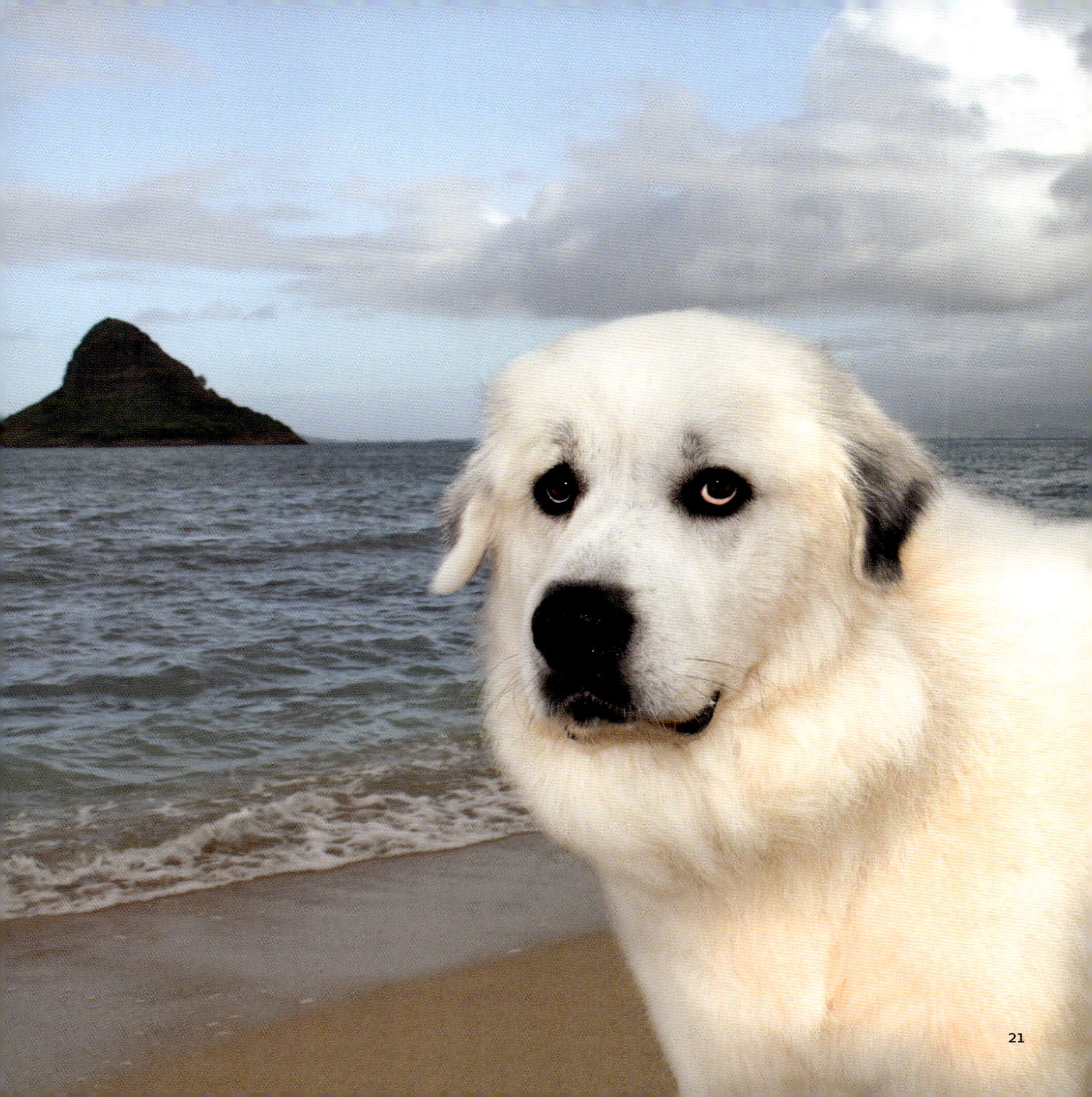

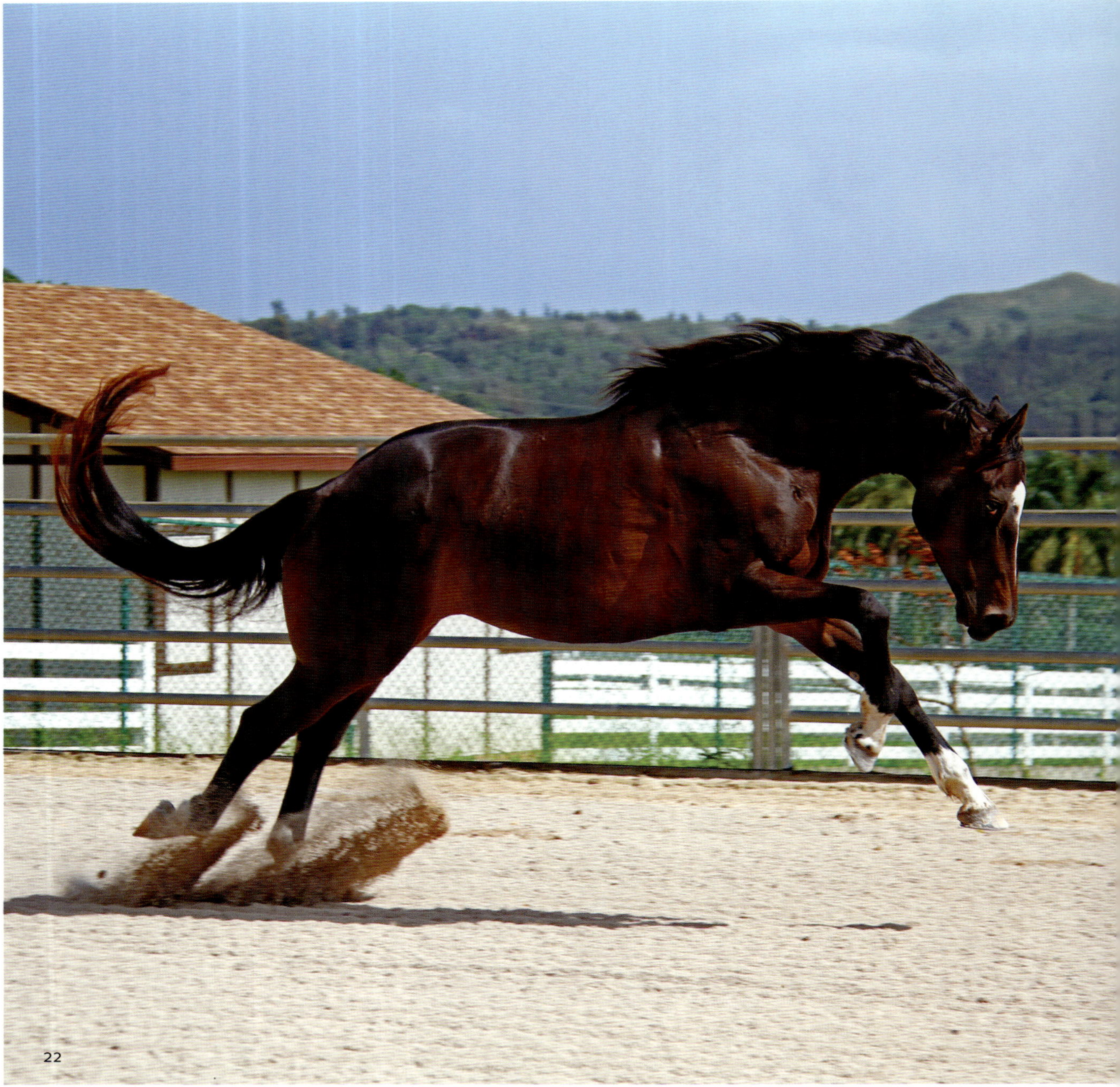

"What a show-off!
Hey, wait a minute!
THAT'S ME."

Tip: Vary your poses. These photos are of the same horse on the same day. Warning: if the active shots are going to result in a very messy pet, you may want to capture the "glam shots" first.

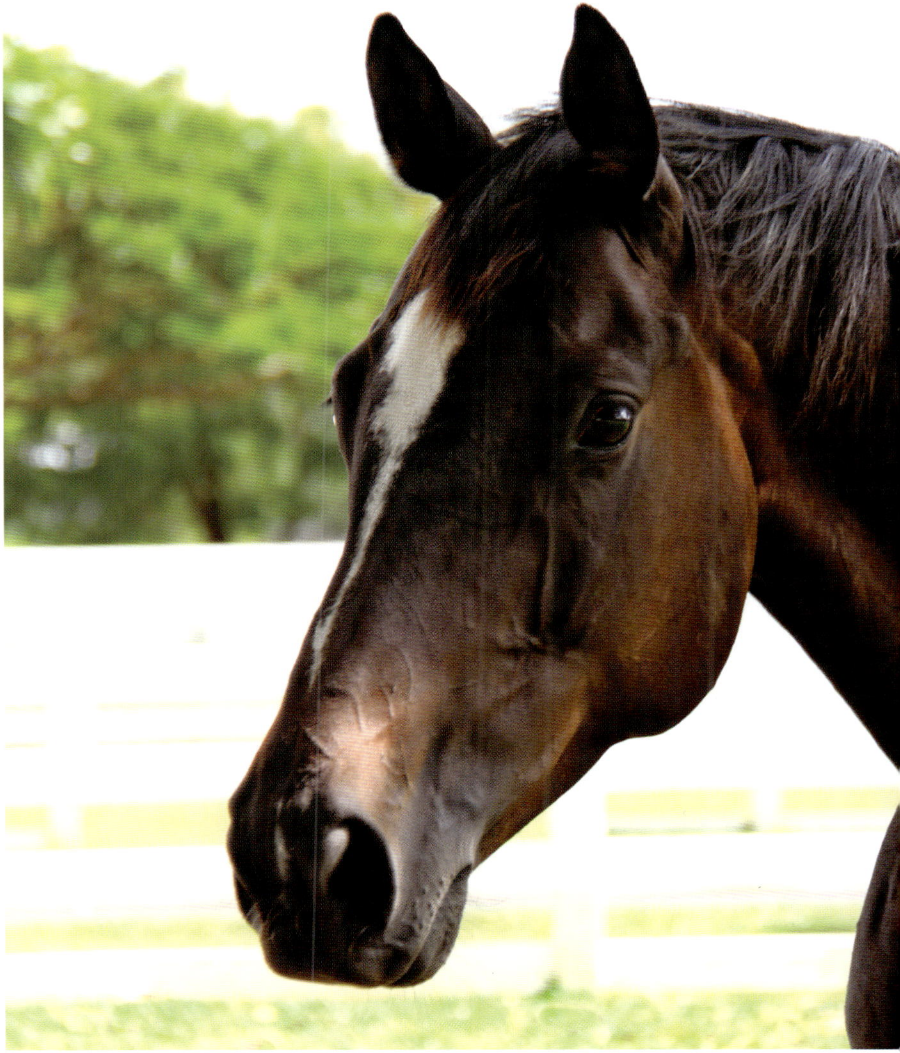

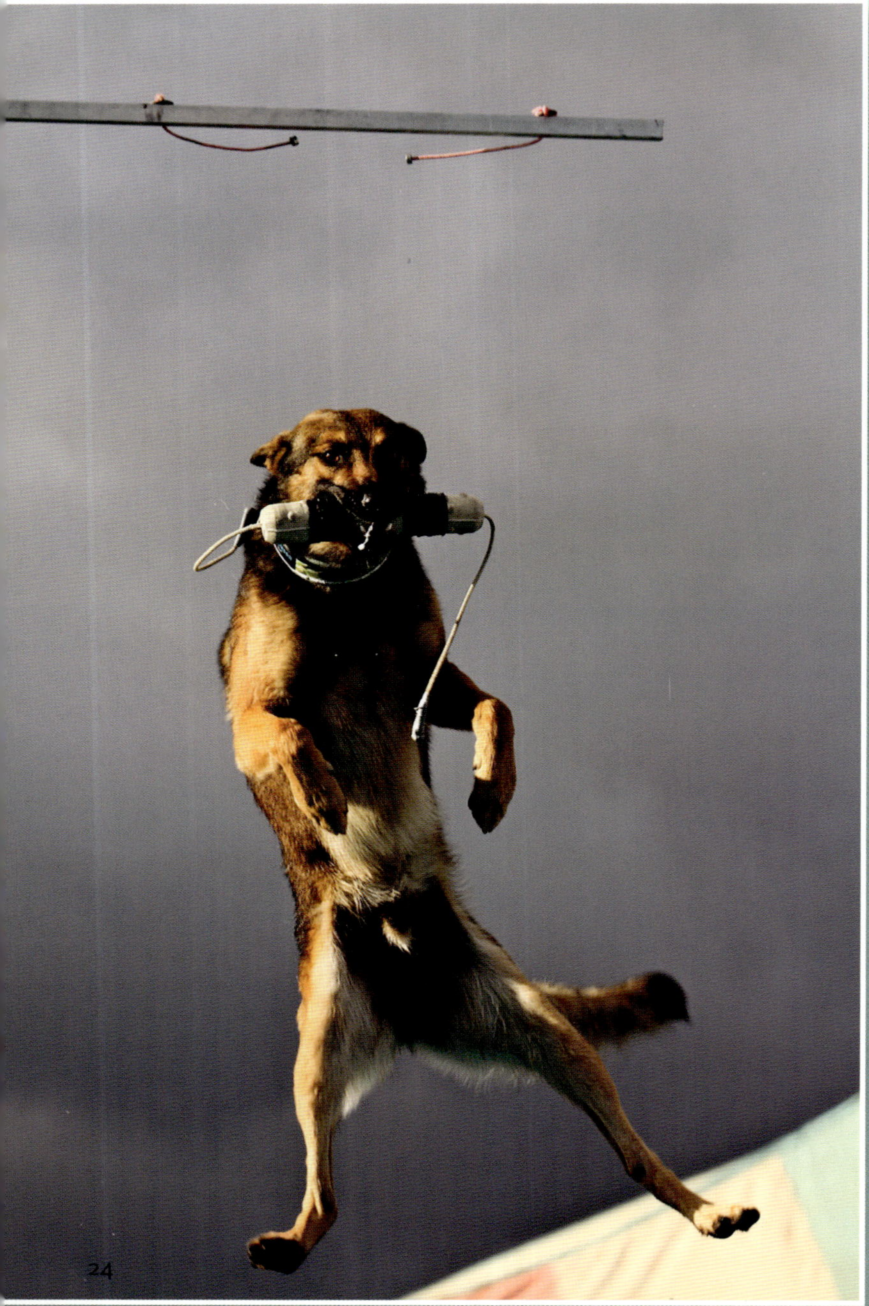

"Well, I'm up here.
Now, how do I get
DOWN?"

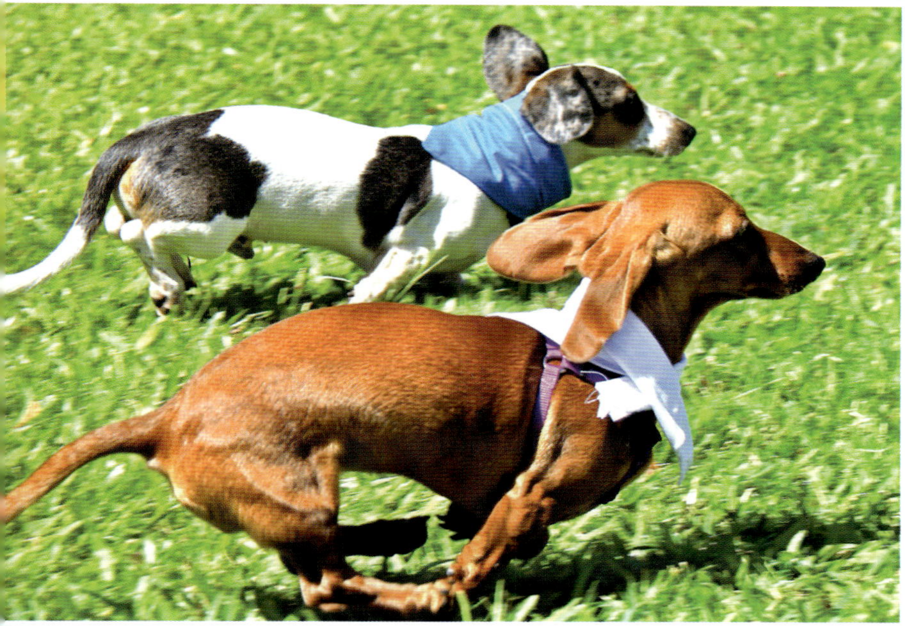

"INCOMING...
RUN!"

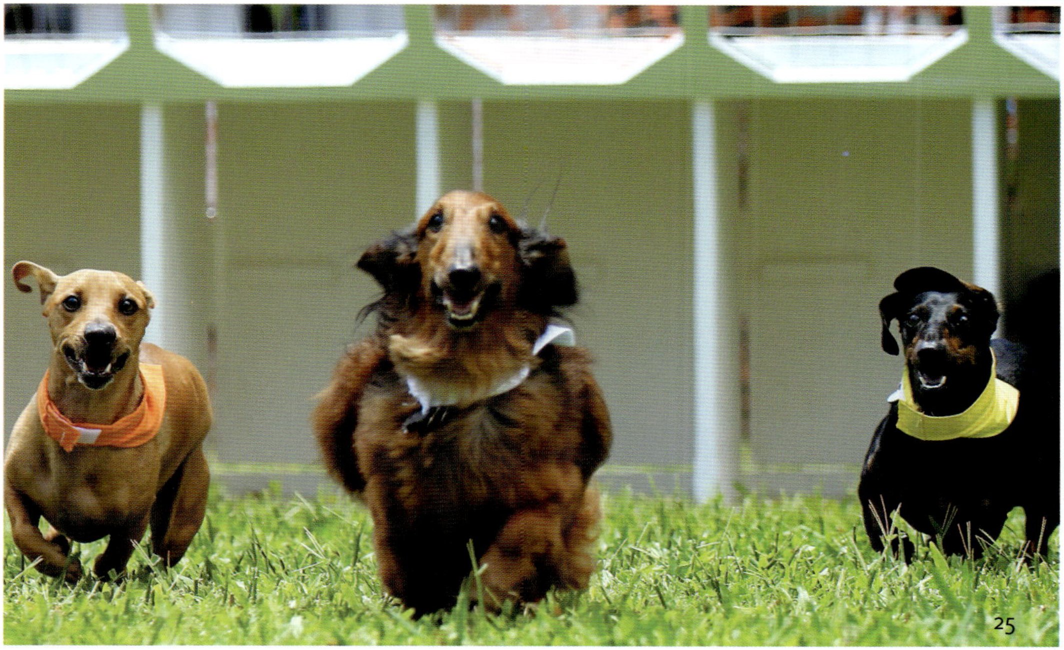

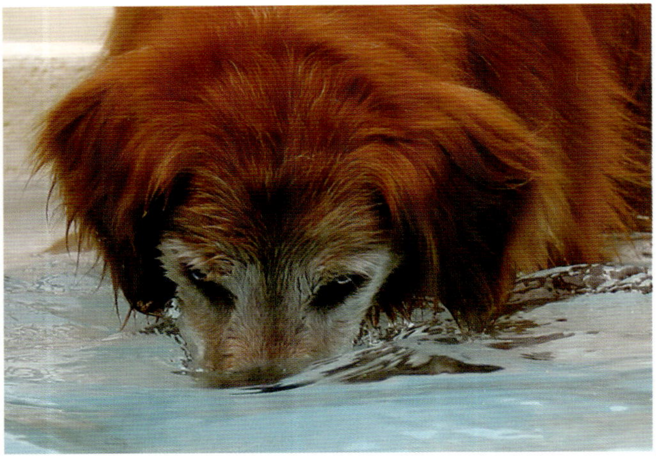

RECIPE FOR A SANDY NOSE:

1. Dip face in water.

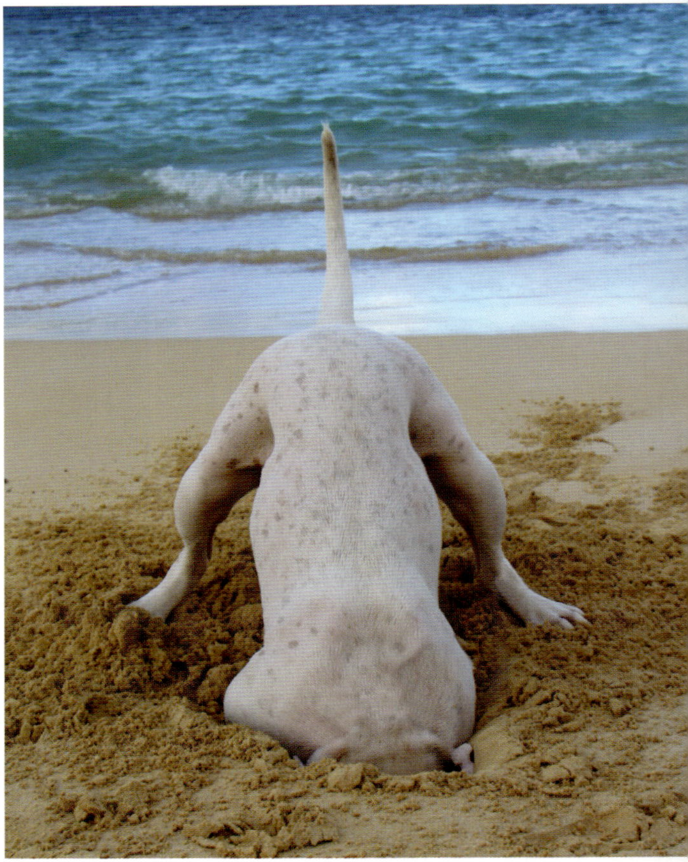

2. Dig deep hole on beach and stick head in.

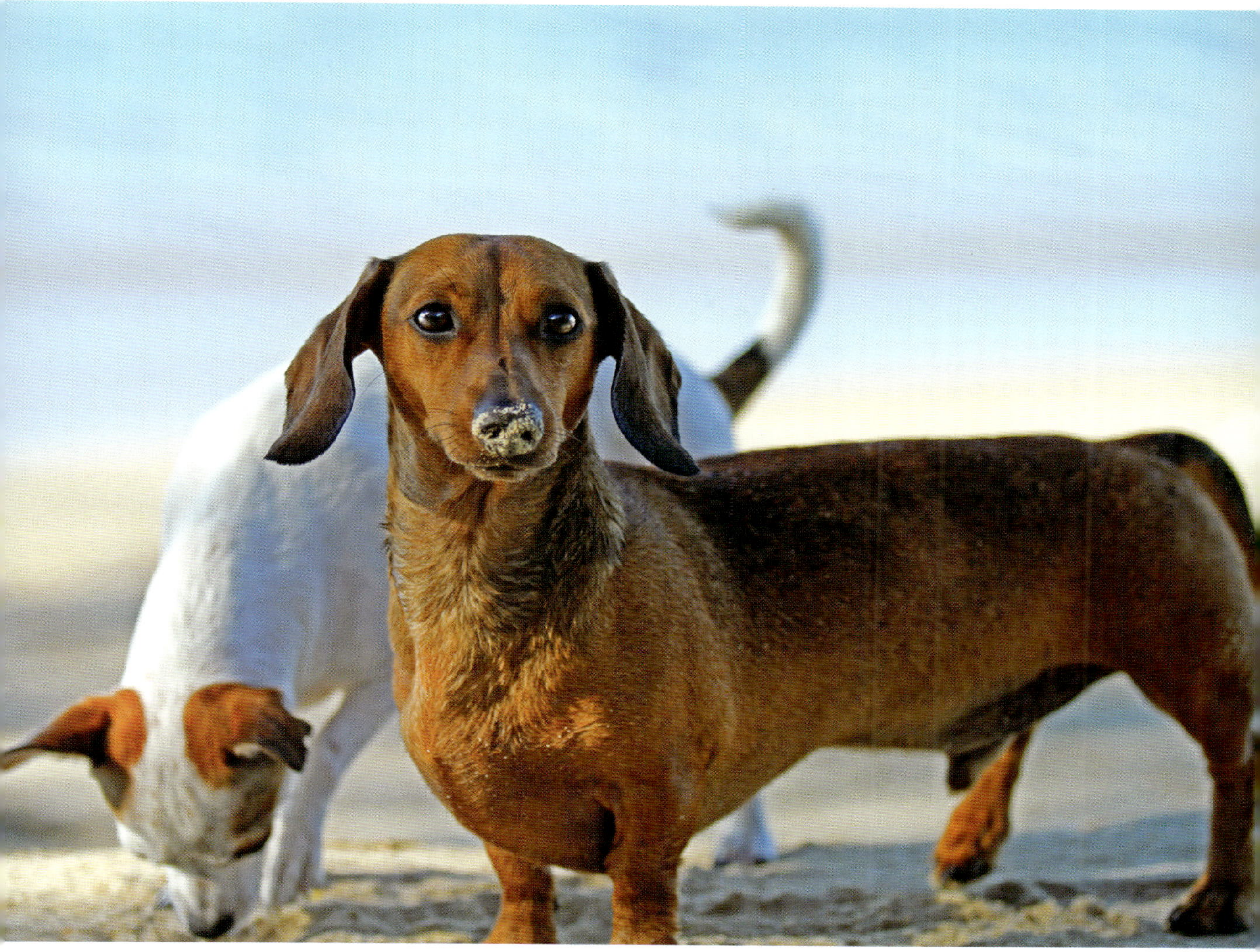

3. Reveal!

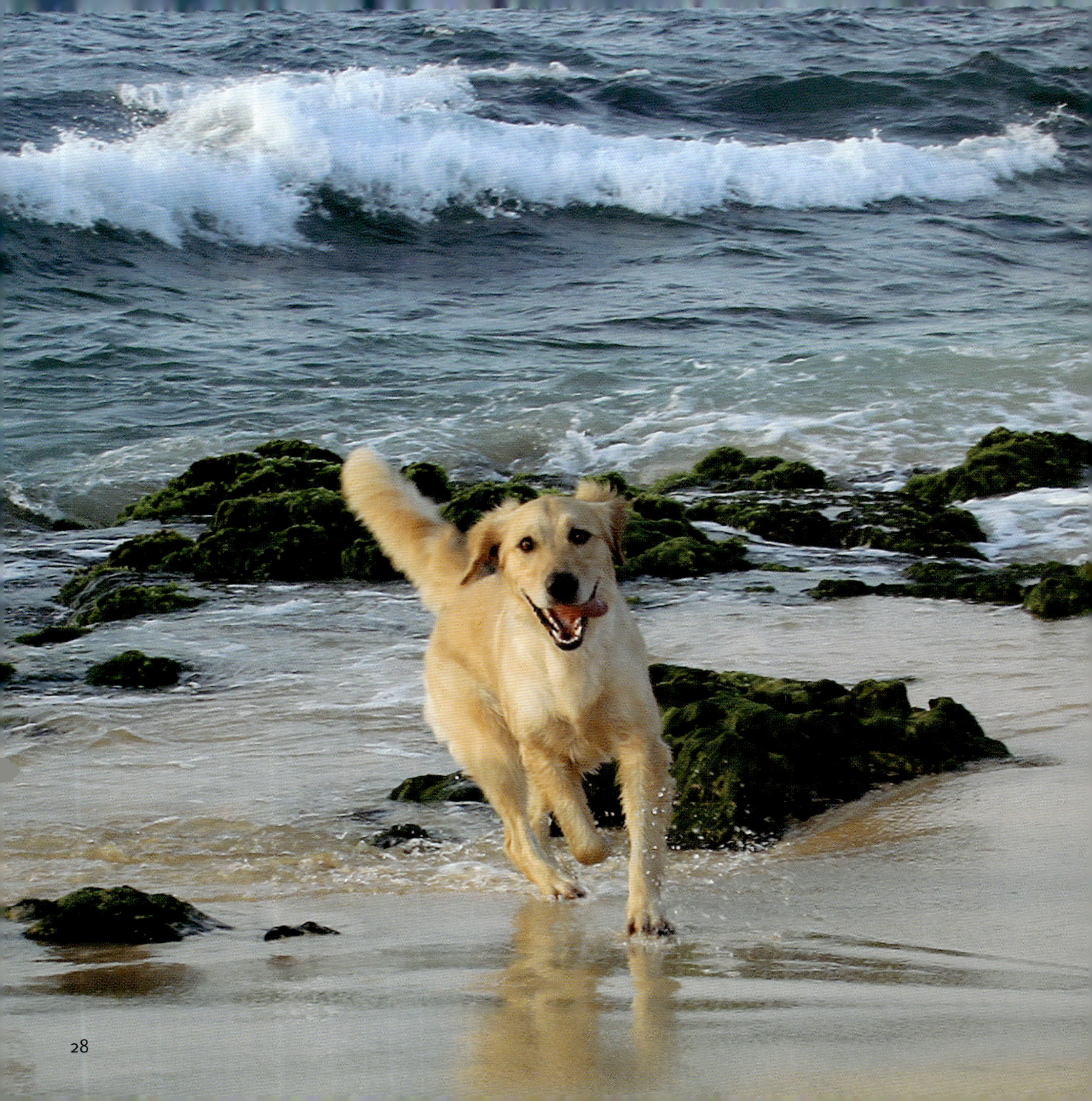

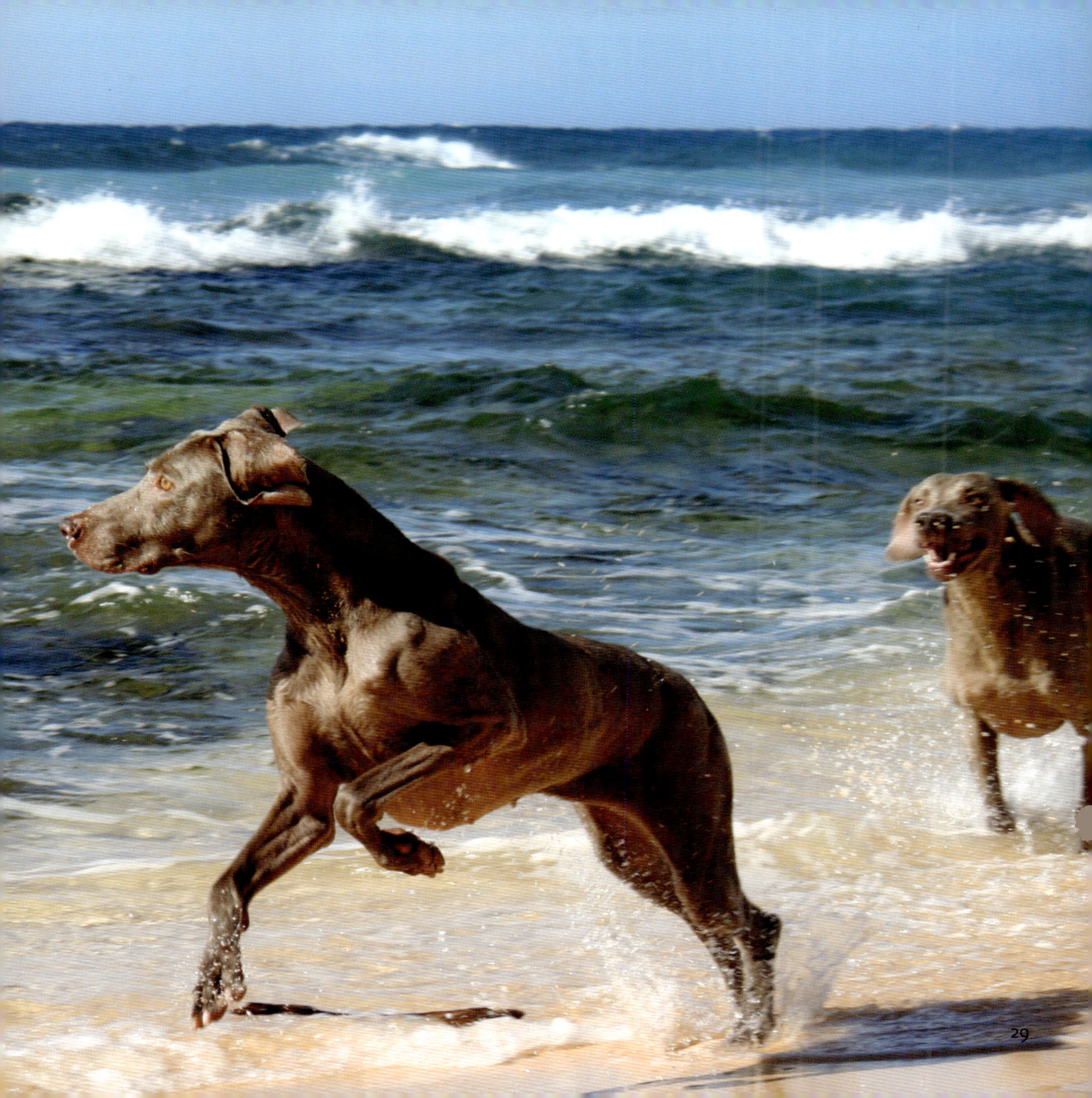

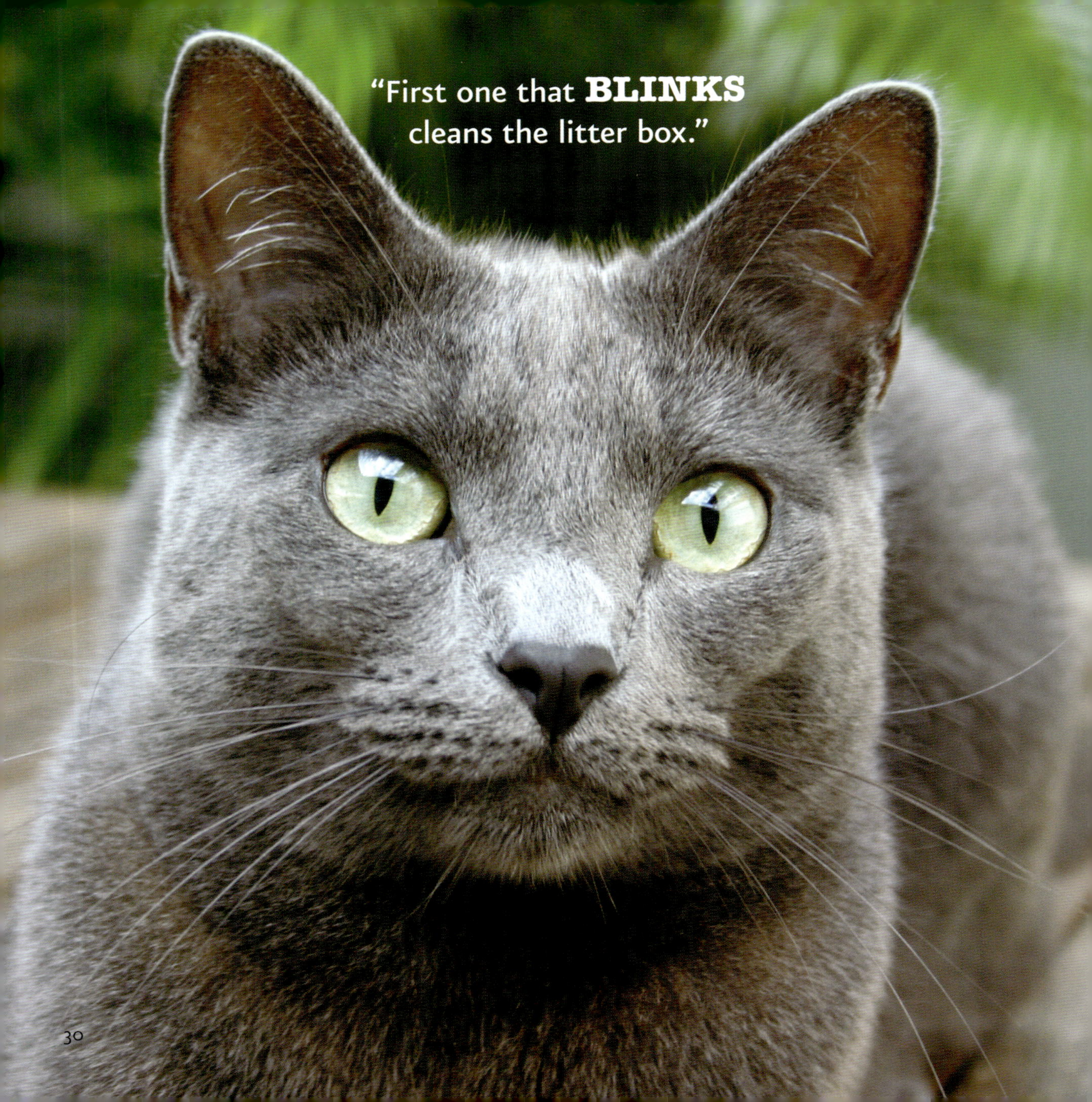

"First one that **BLINKS** cleans the litter box."

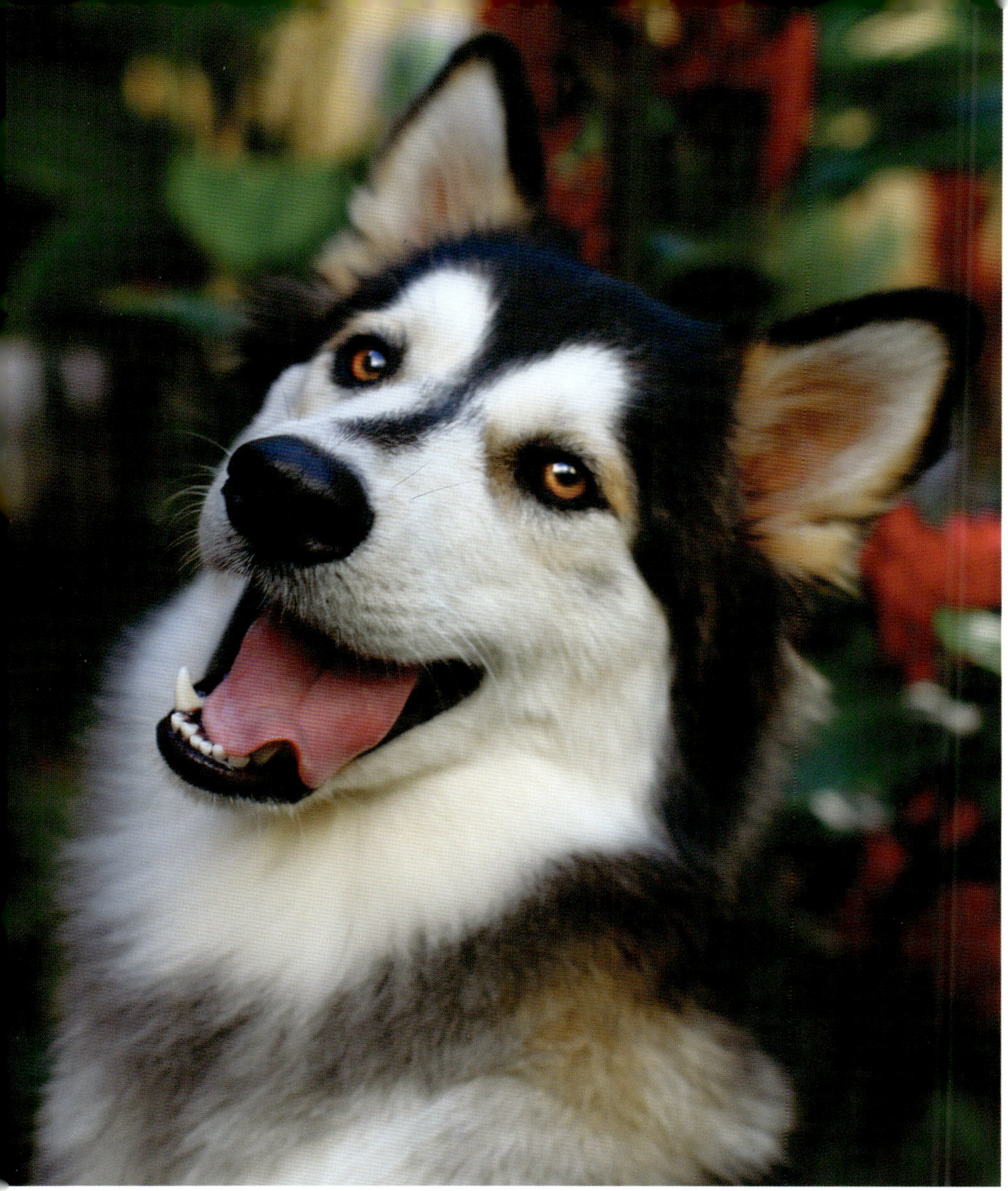

Tip: Photographing your pet in familiar places serves two purposes. First, your pet will be less distracted. Second, when you think of your pet, these are the places that you most likely see them in your "mind's eye."

"You say **'DIVA'** like it's a bad thing."

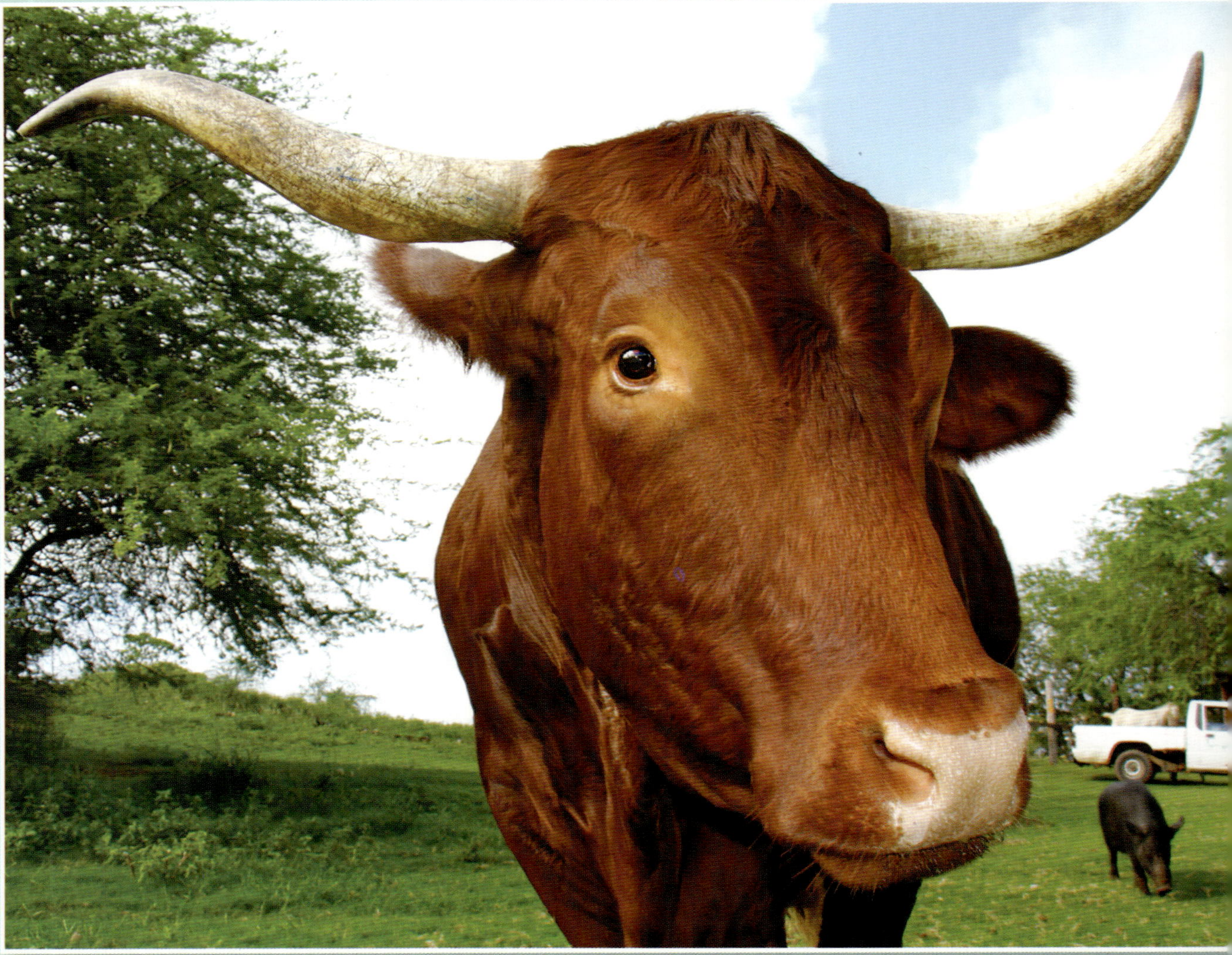

"GOT MILK?"

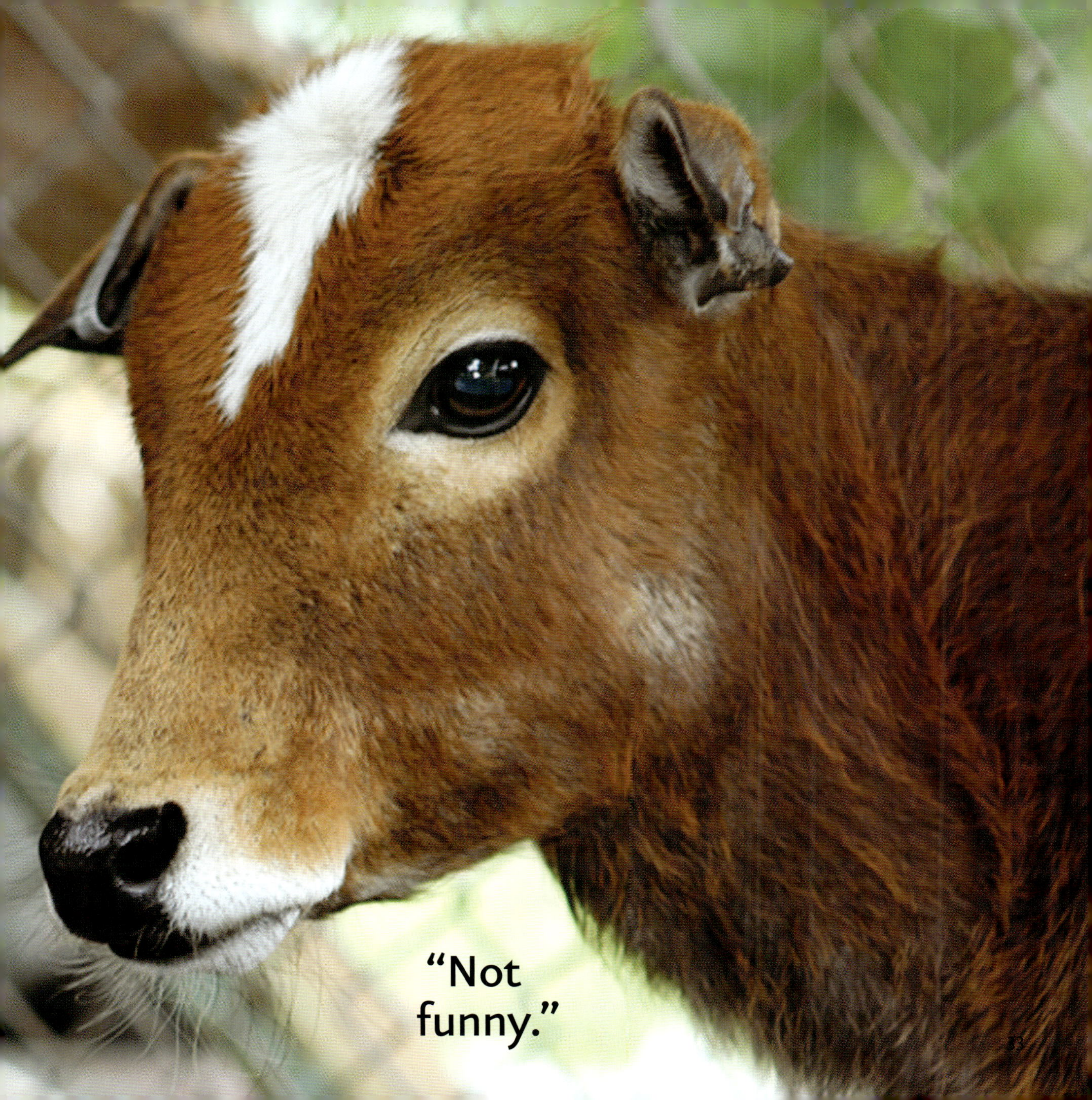

“Not
funny.”

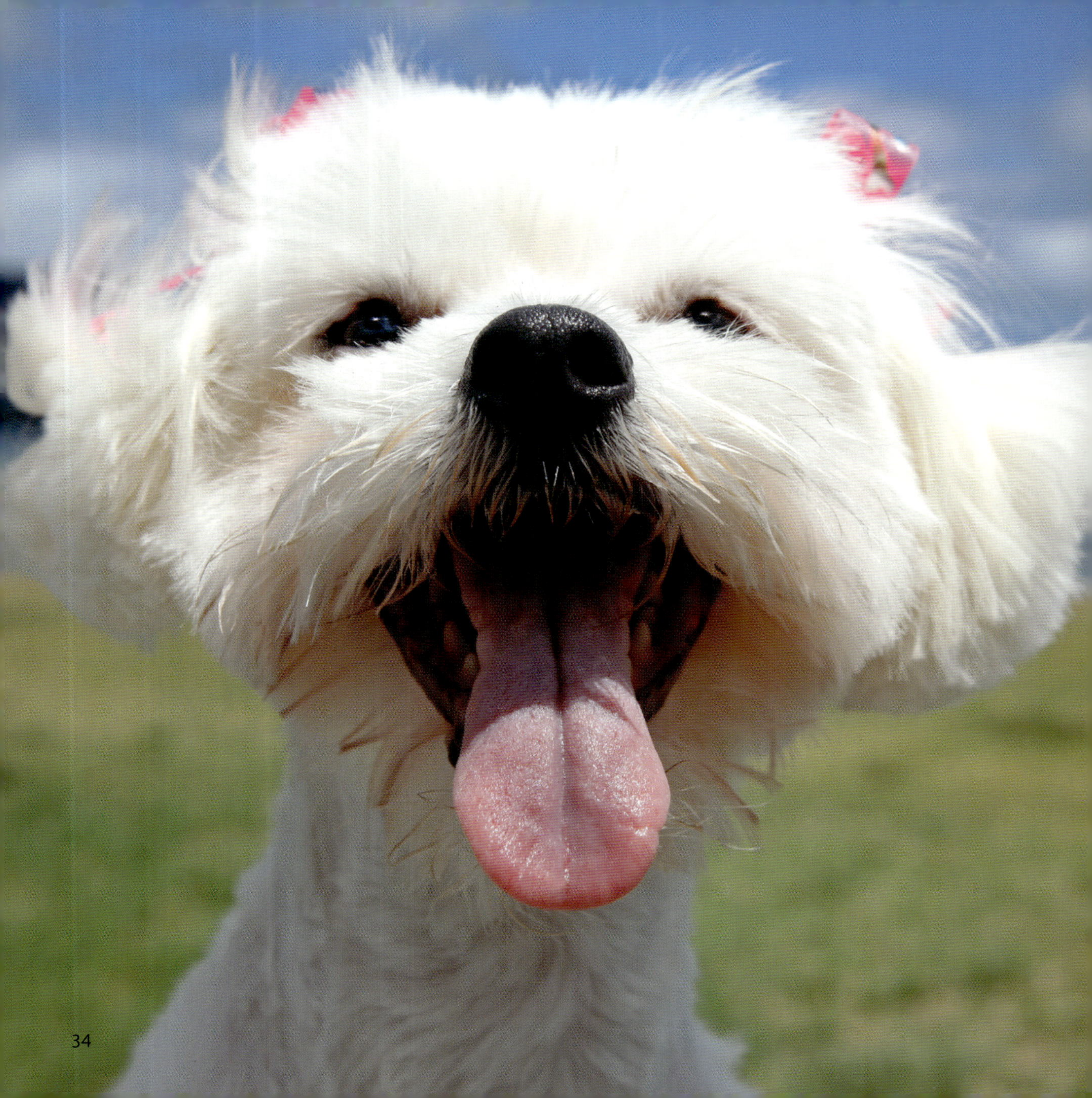

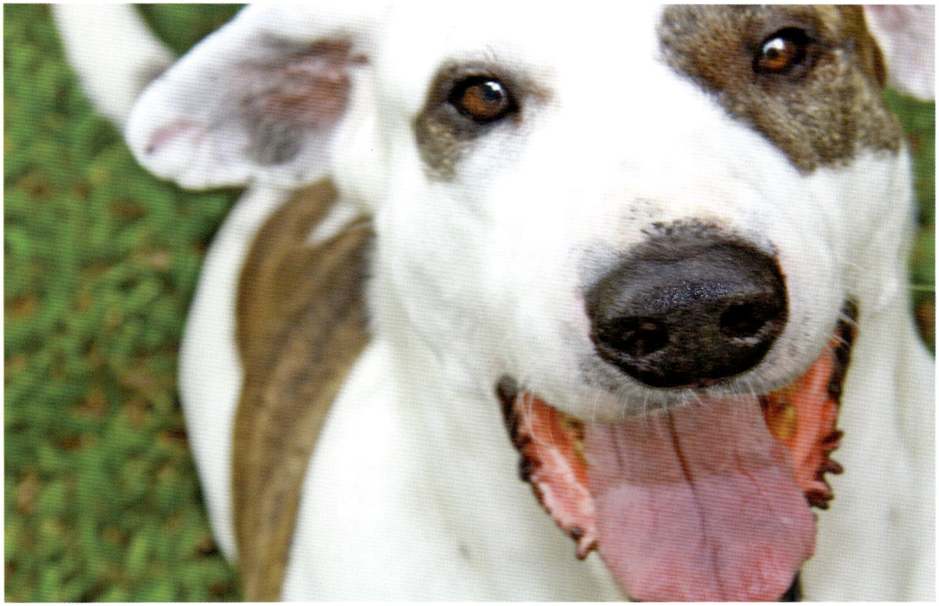

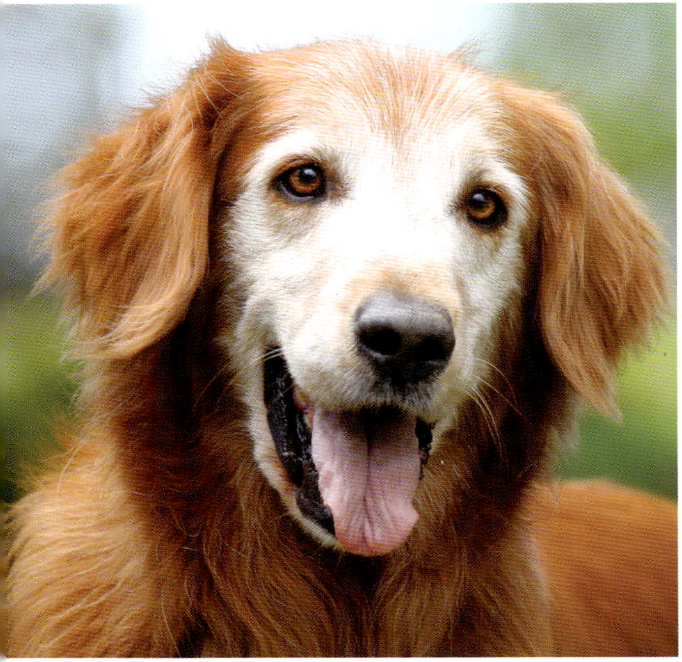

“EXCUSE ME, EXCUSE ME!

Do I have something on my tongue?”

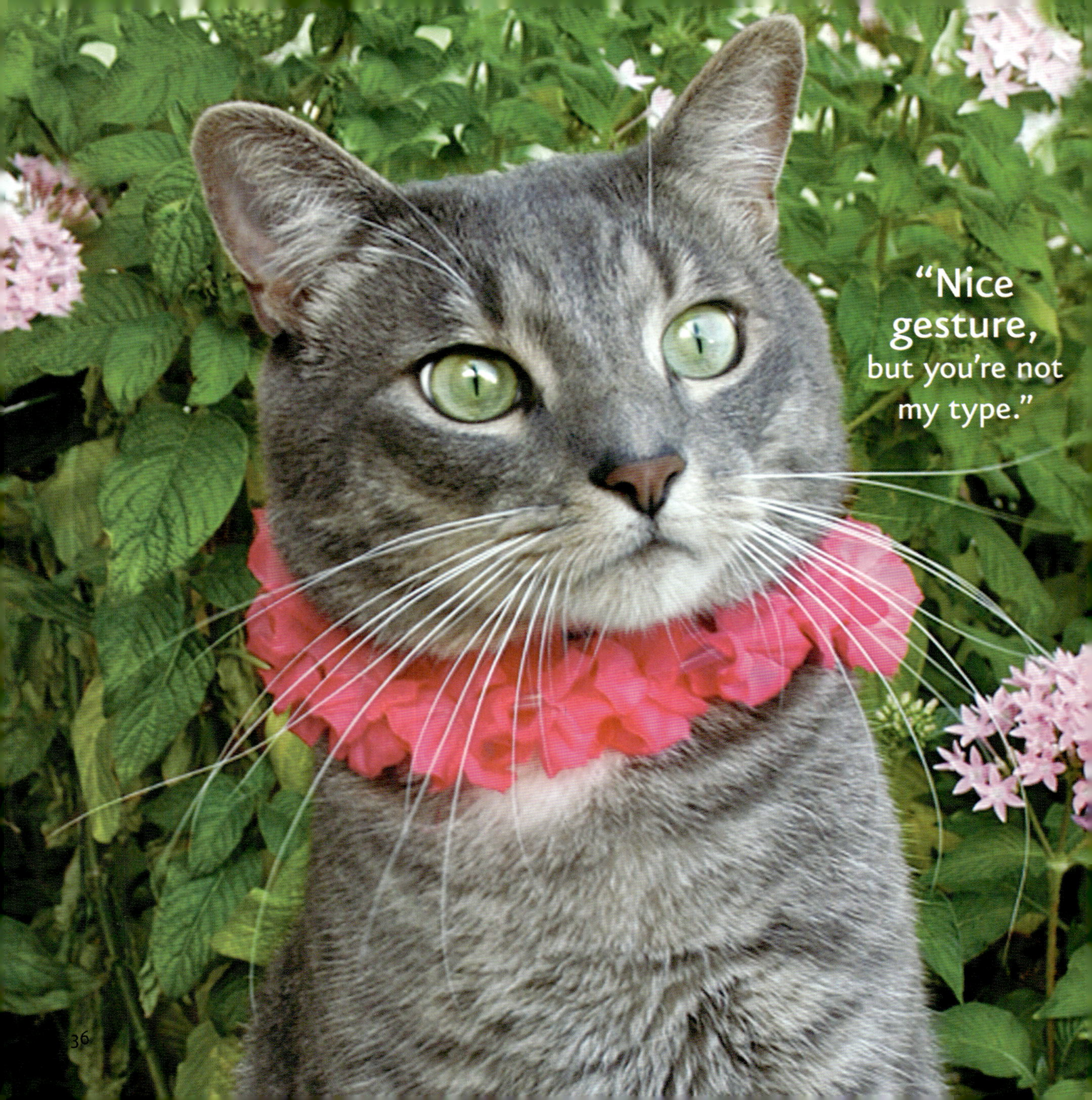

"Nice gesture, but you're not my type."

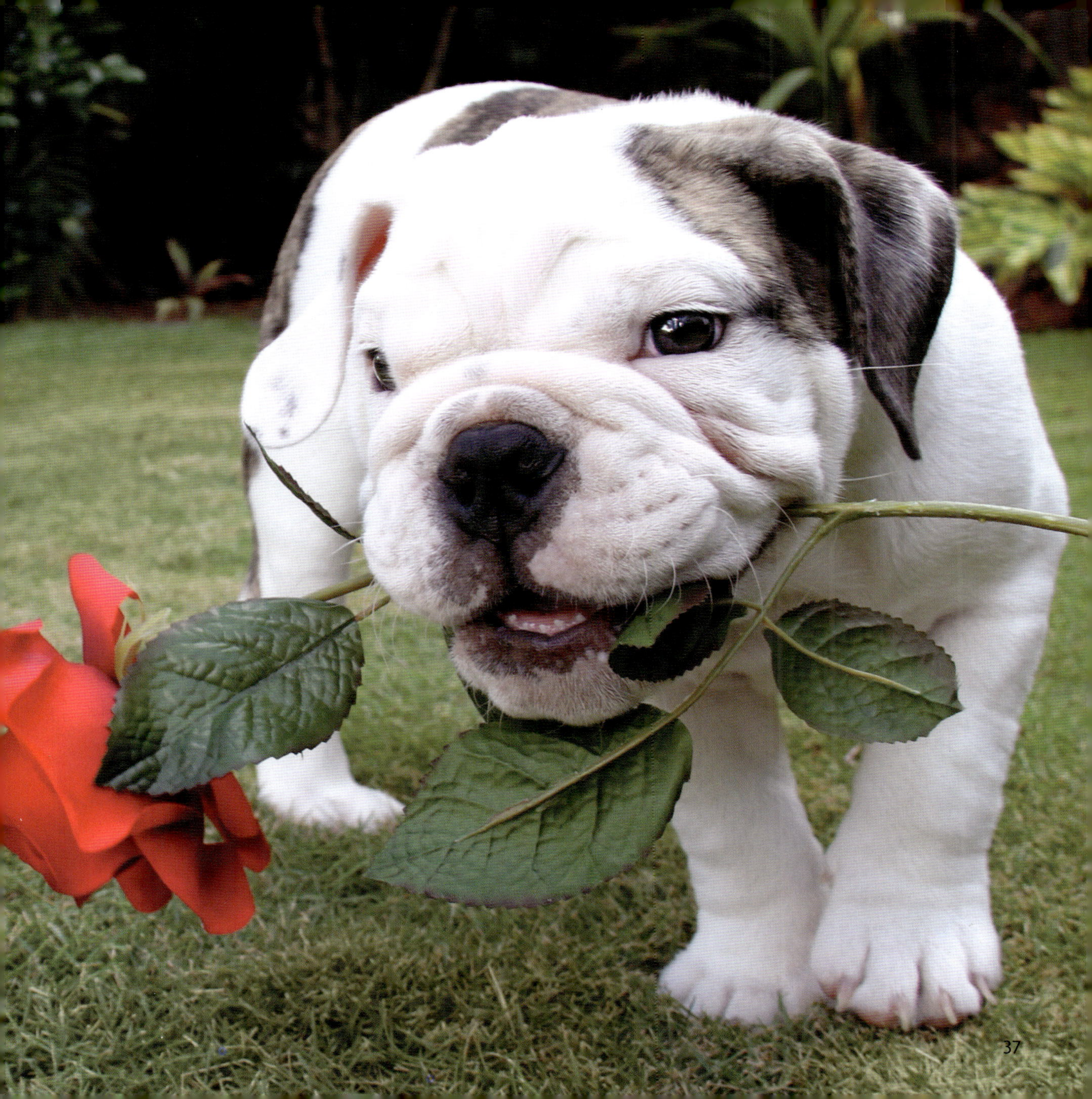

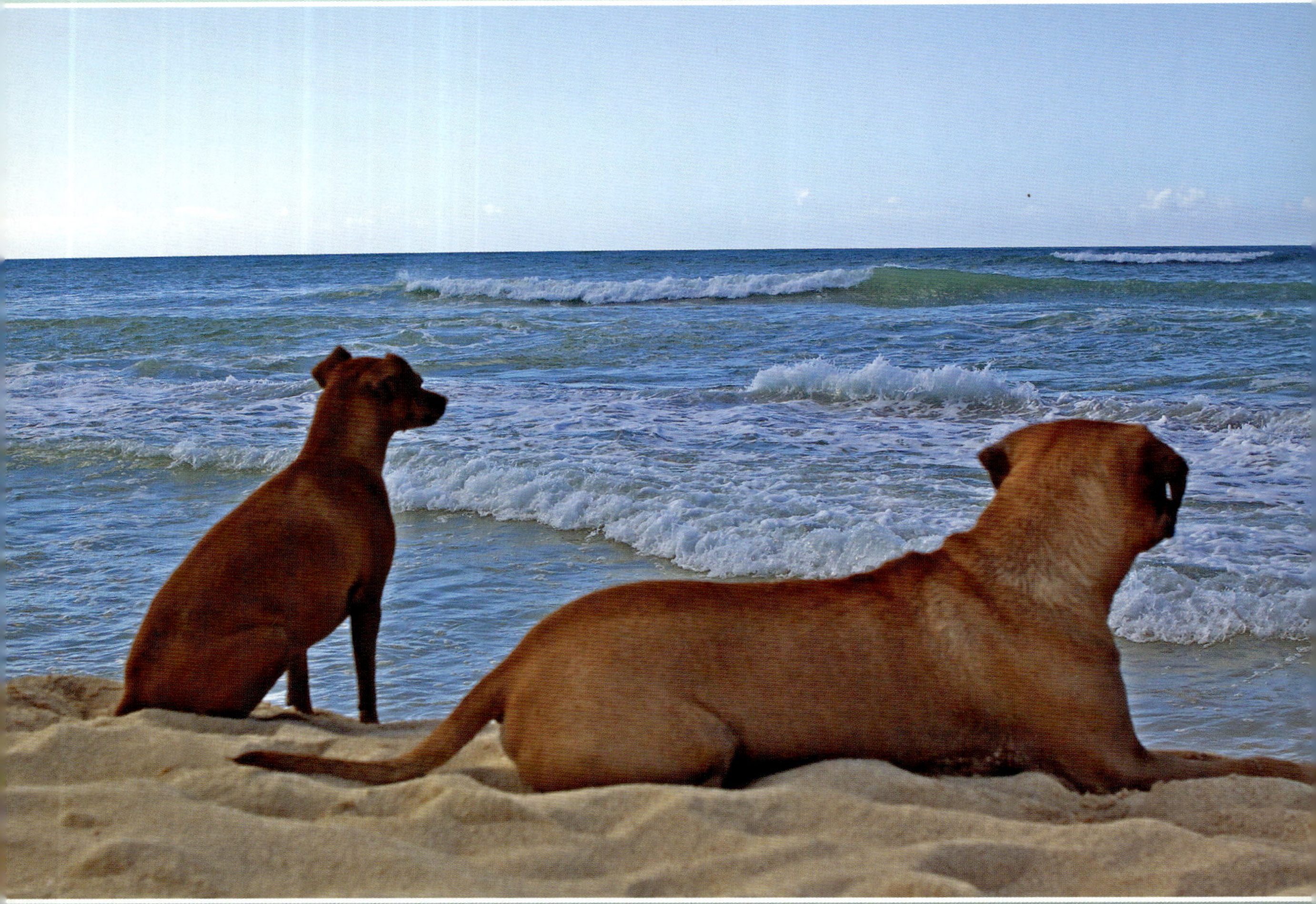

"That tennis ball isn't getting
ANY CLOSER, Sparky..."

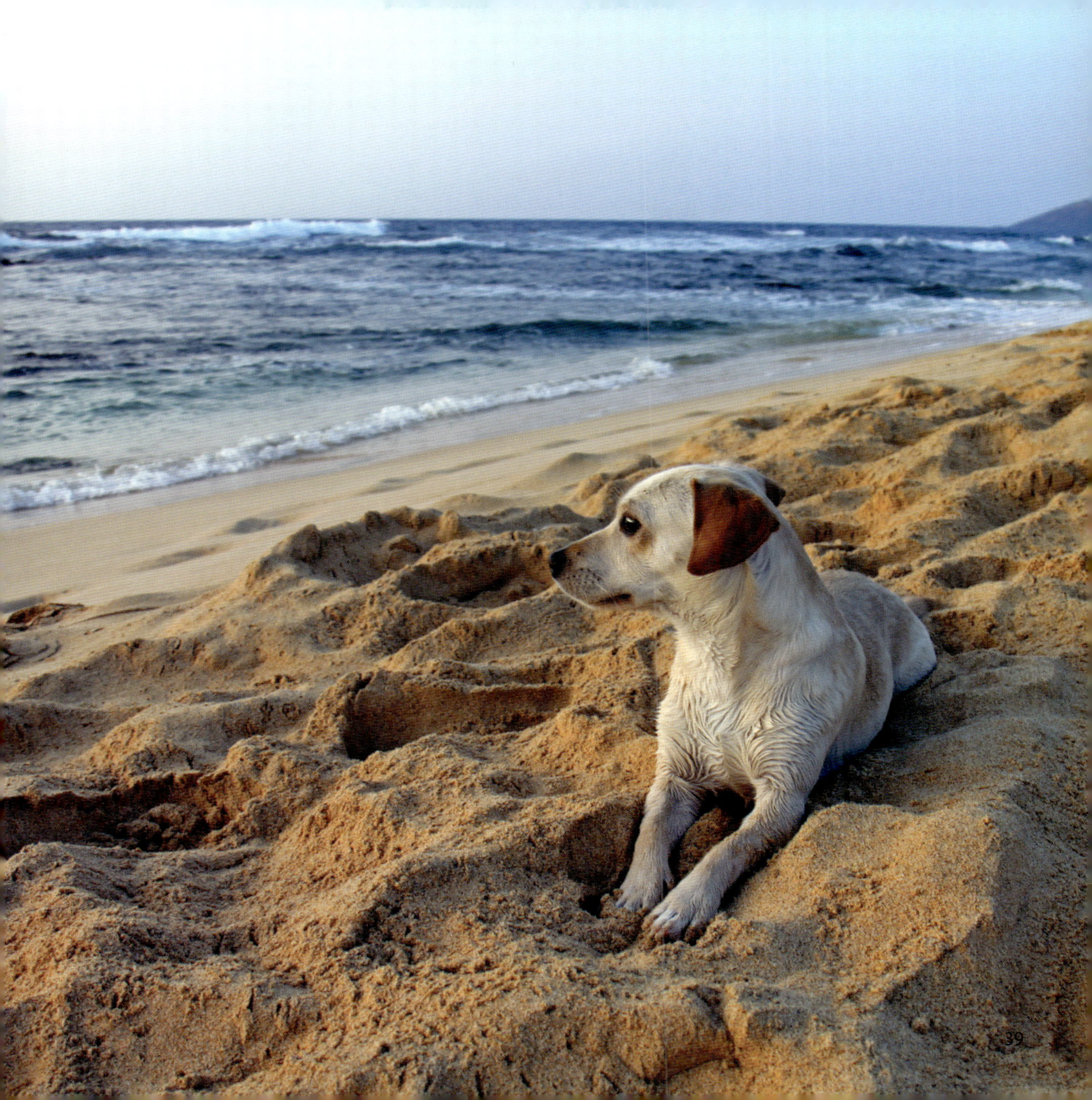

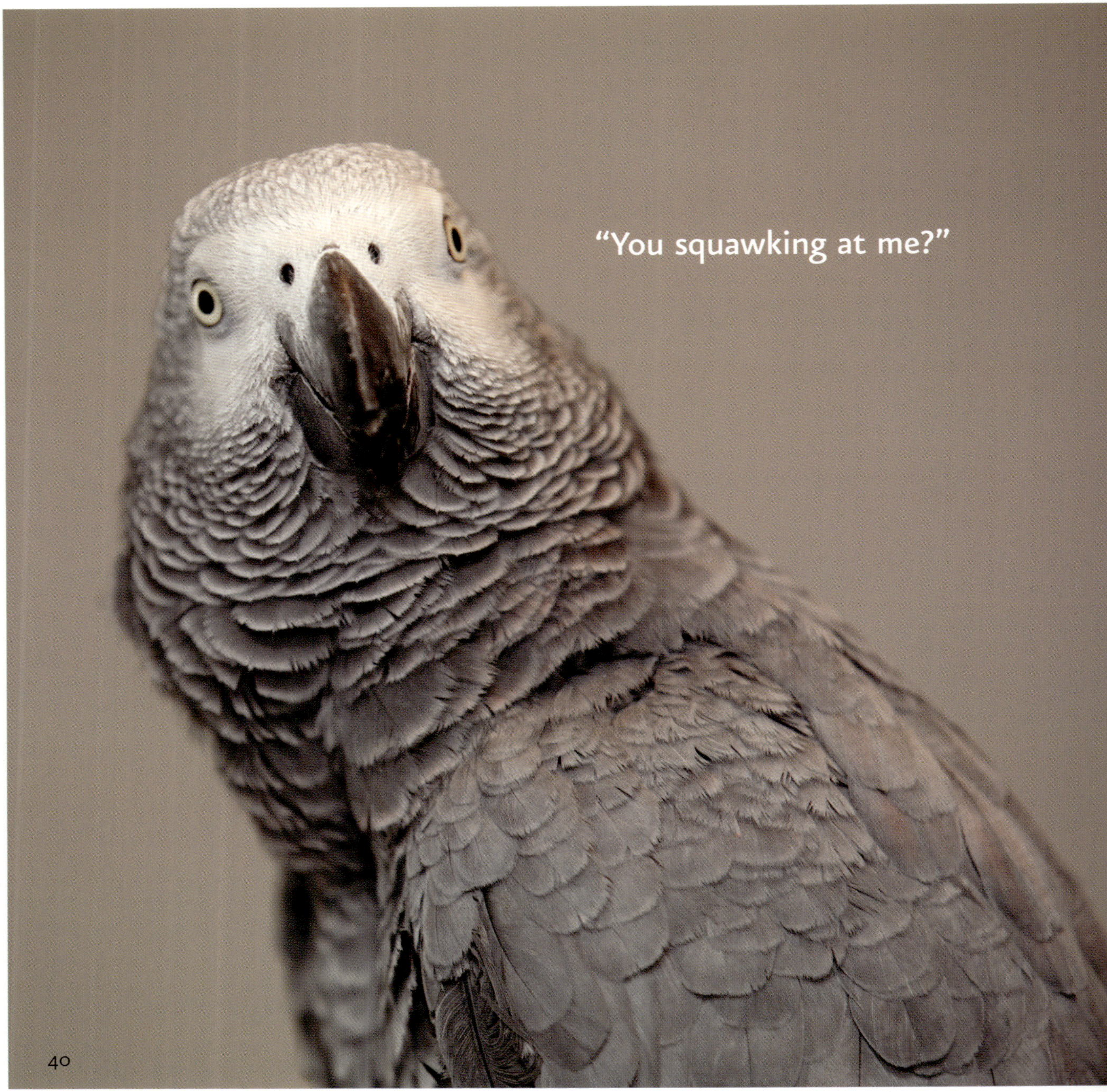

"You squawking at me?"

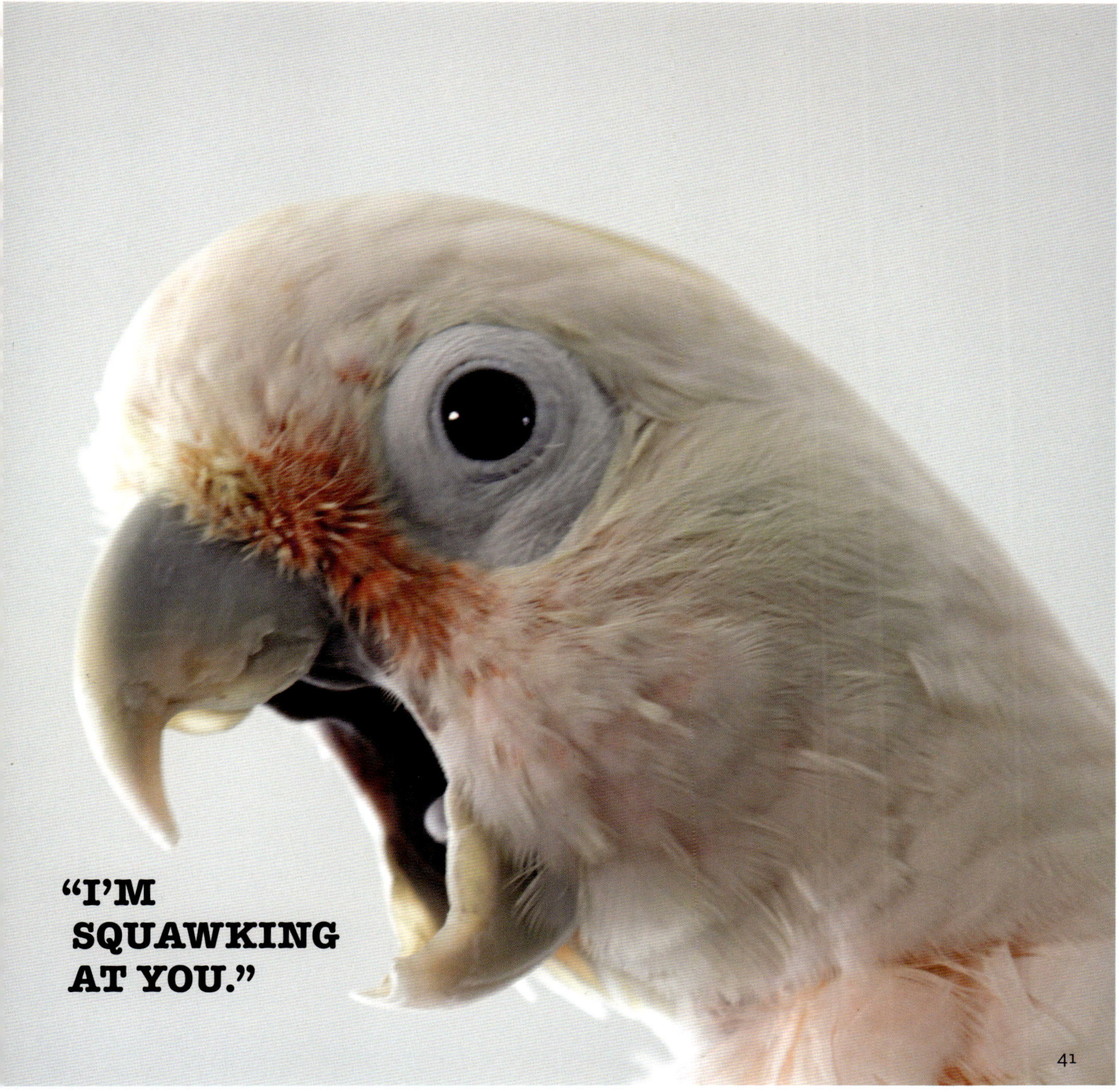
"I'M
SQUAWKING
AT YOU."

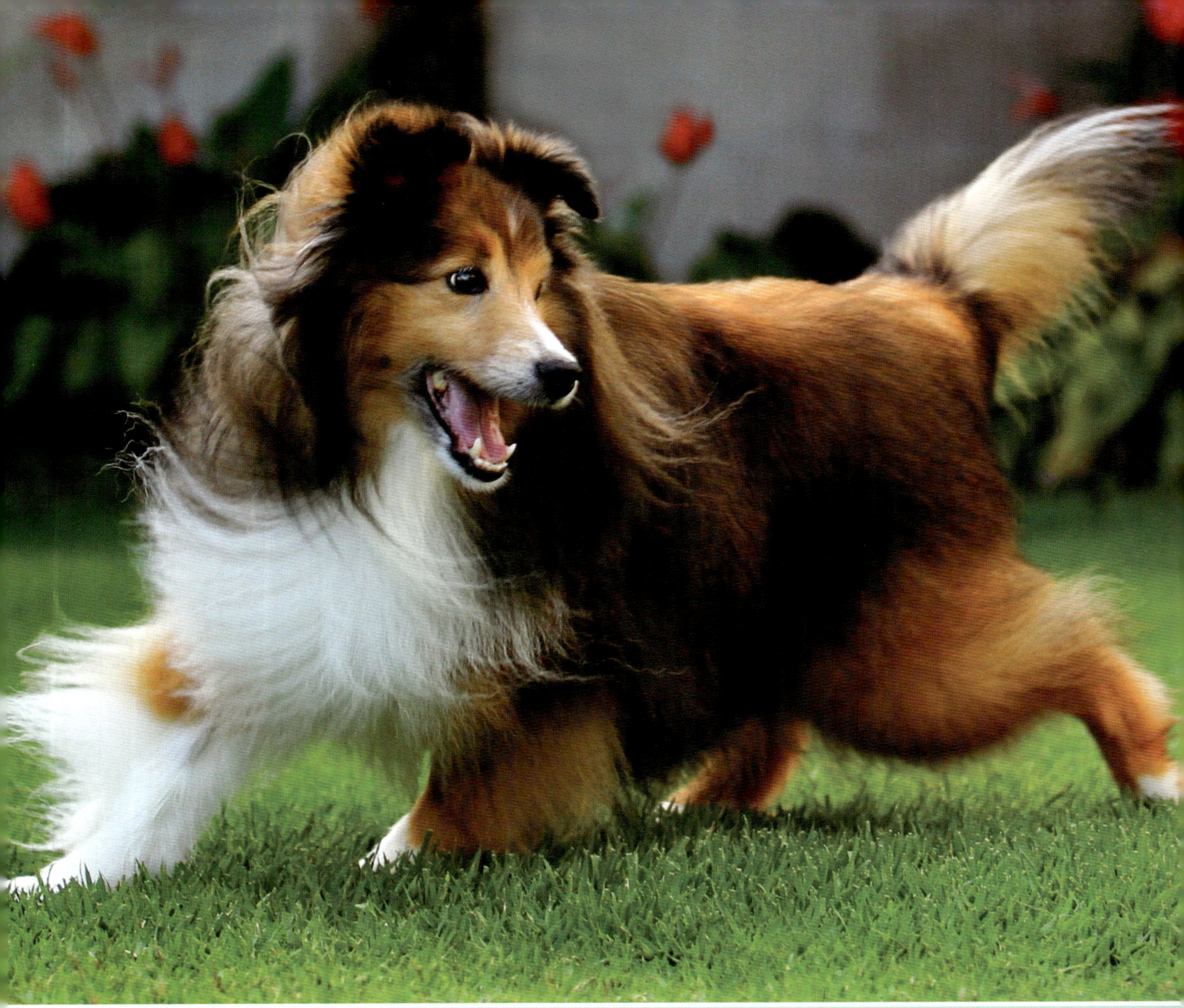

"You didn't actually **PAY**
for that haircut, did you?"

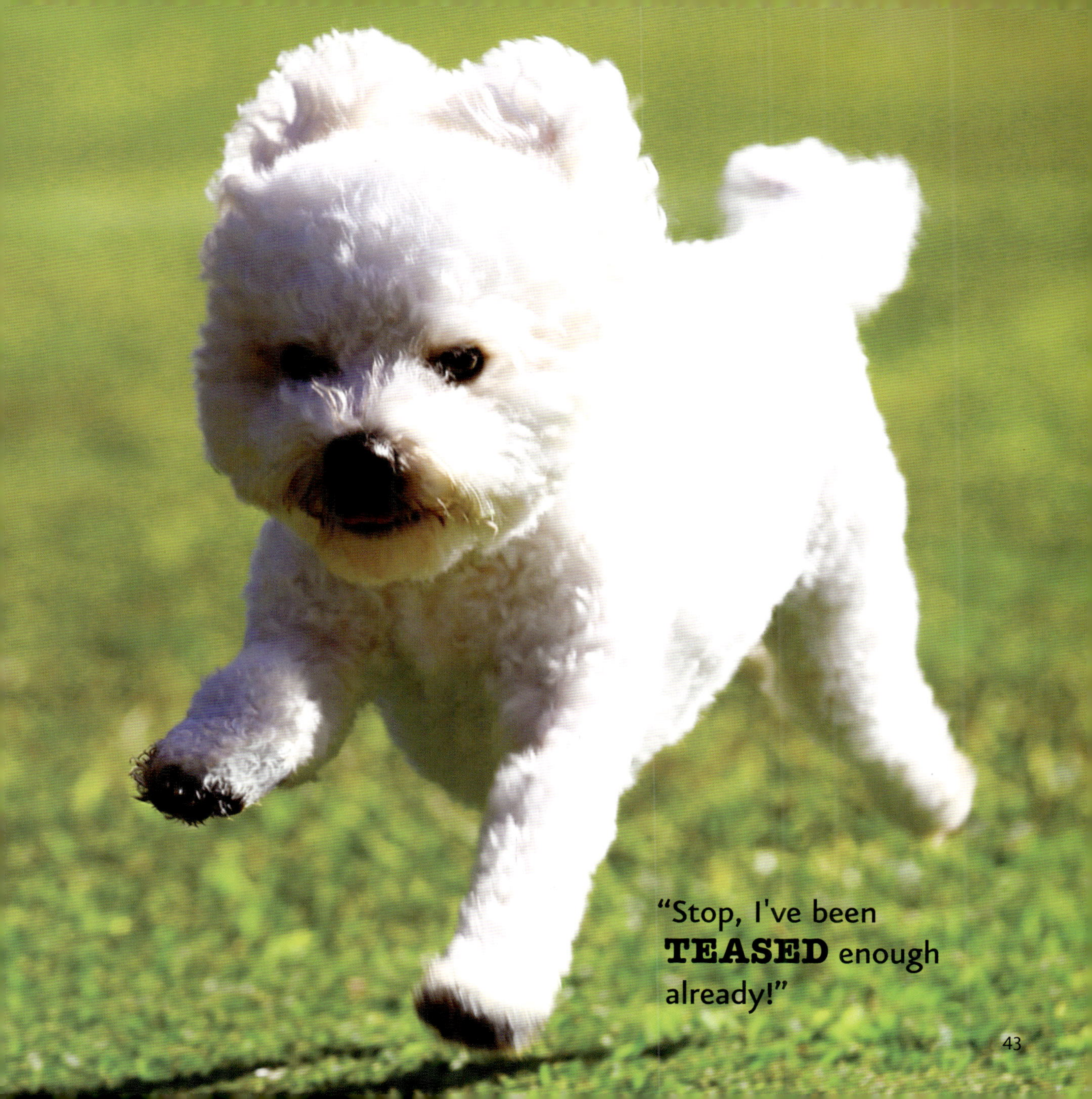

"Stop, I've been **TEASED** enough already!"

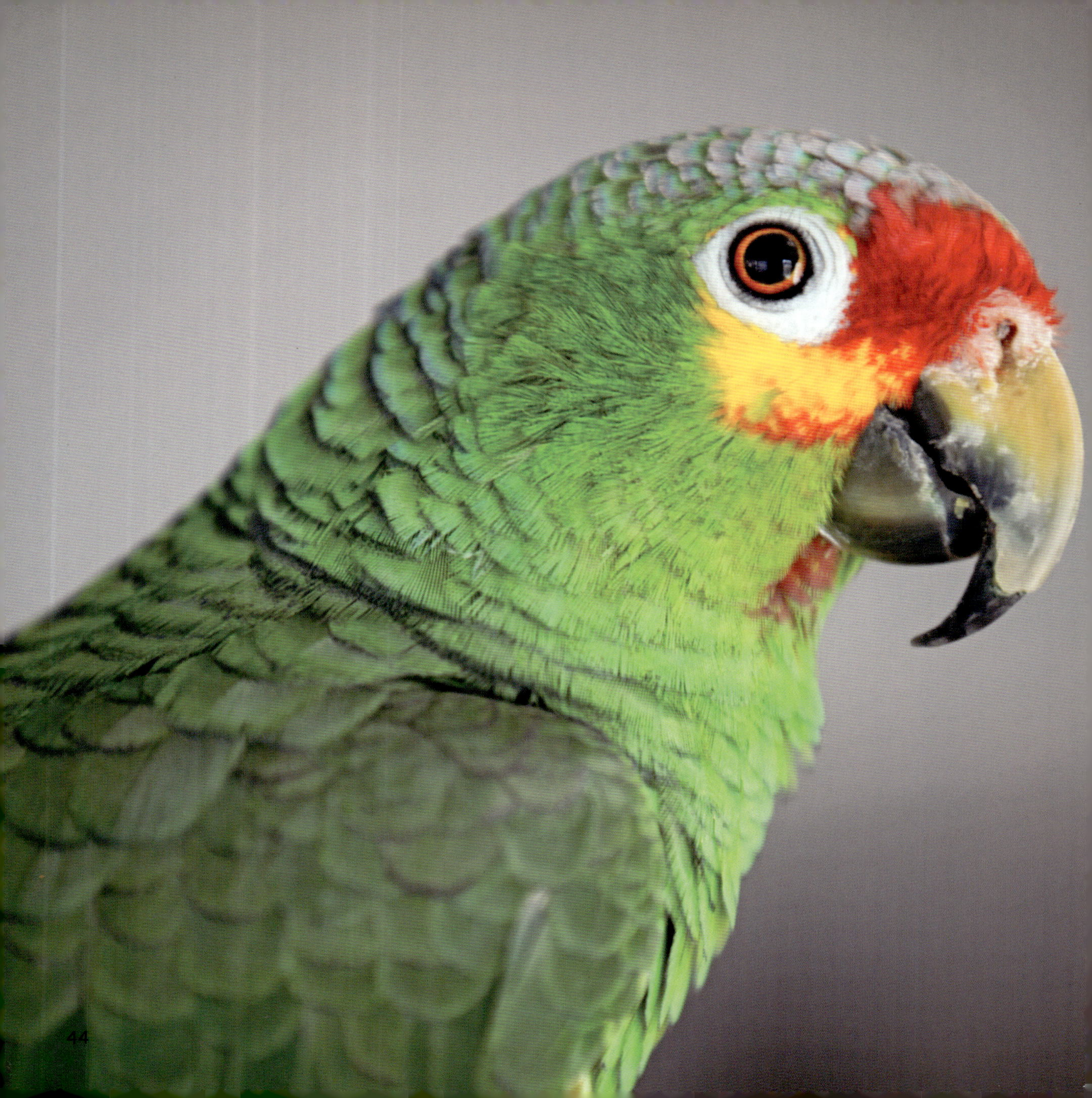

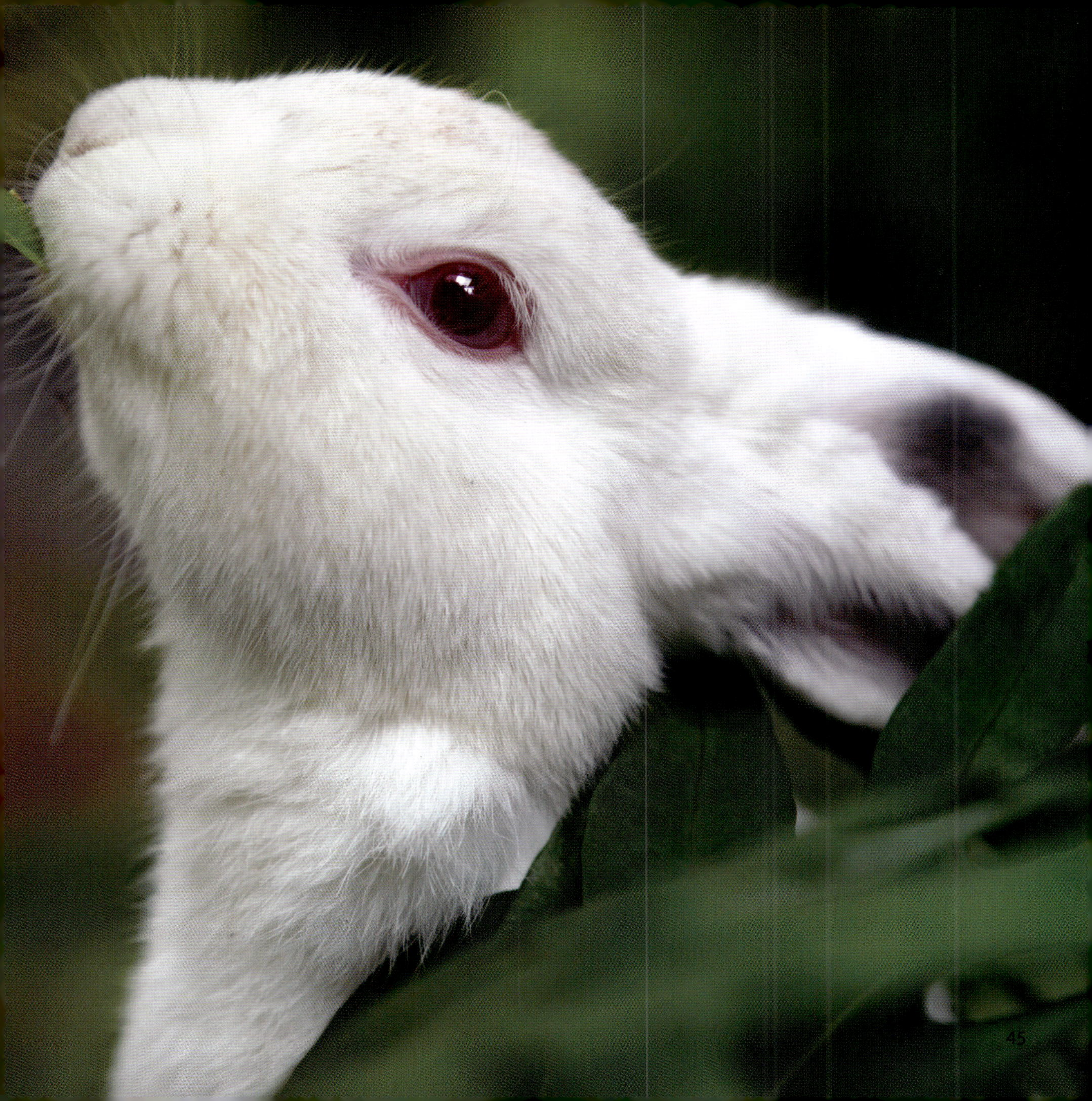

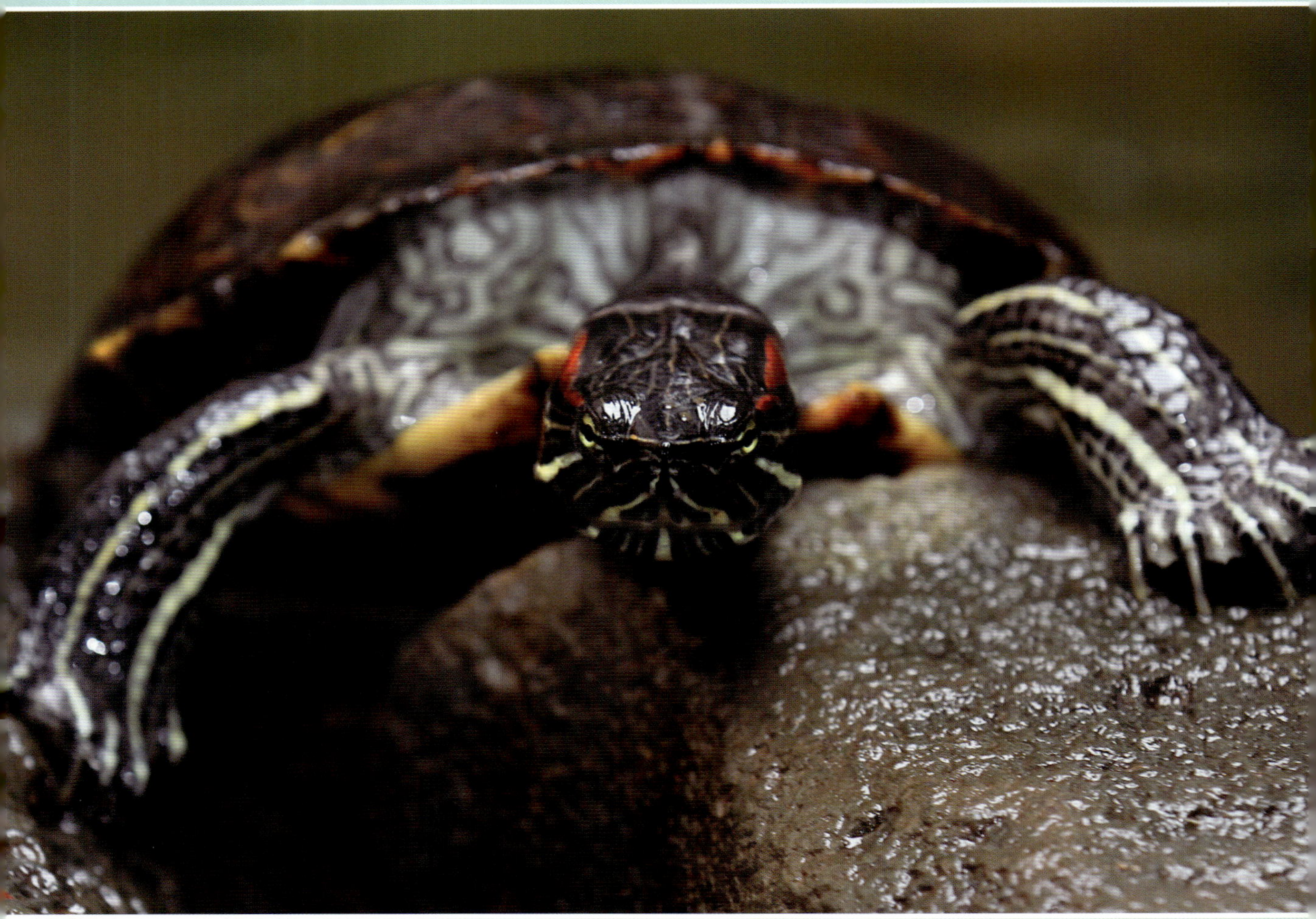

"We prefer to think of ourselves as having
NO NEED TO EVOLVE."

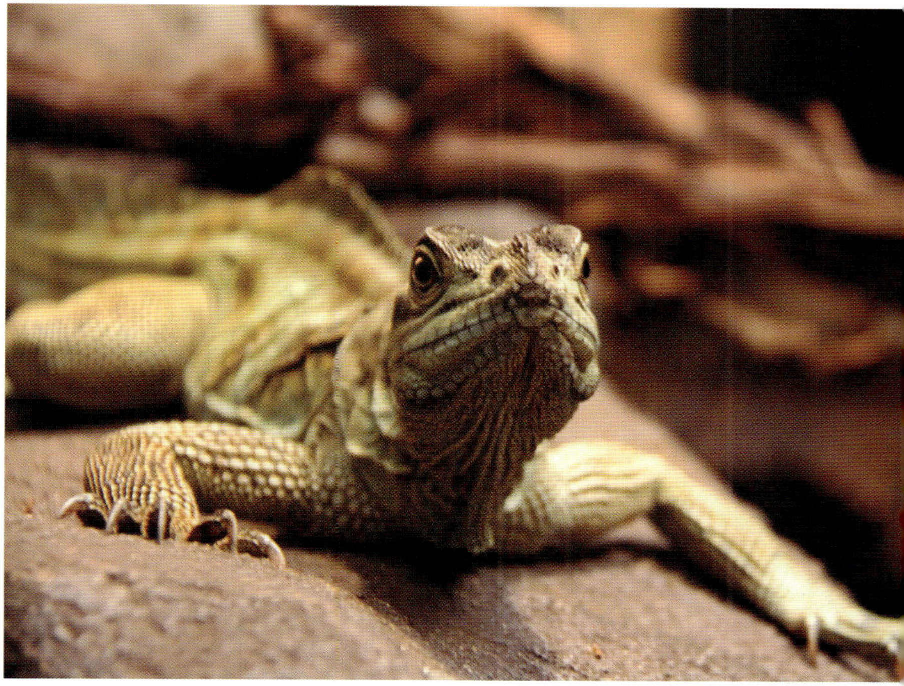

Tip: Note to the would-be pet photographers: the scaly and slimy friends can be quite photogenic as well.

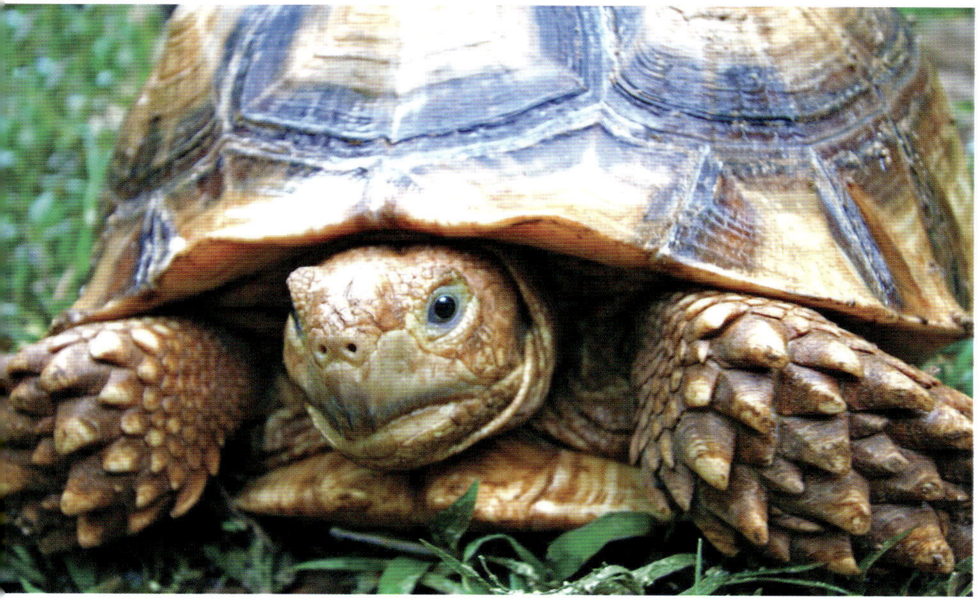

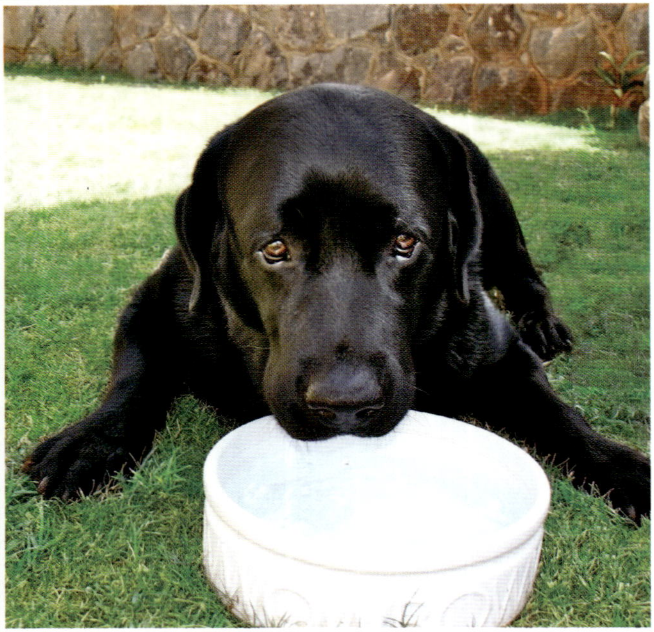

"I could share, but **WHY?**"

"Do you think they could splurge for a **SECOND BOWL?**"

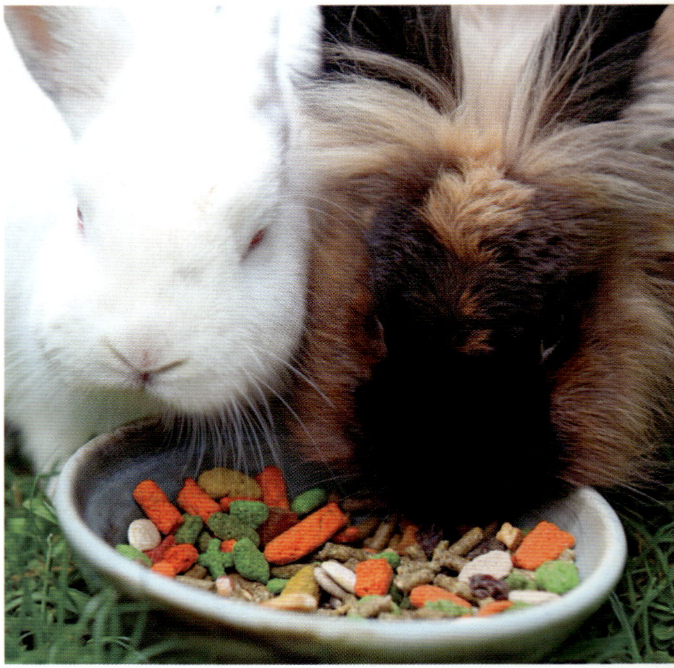

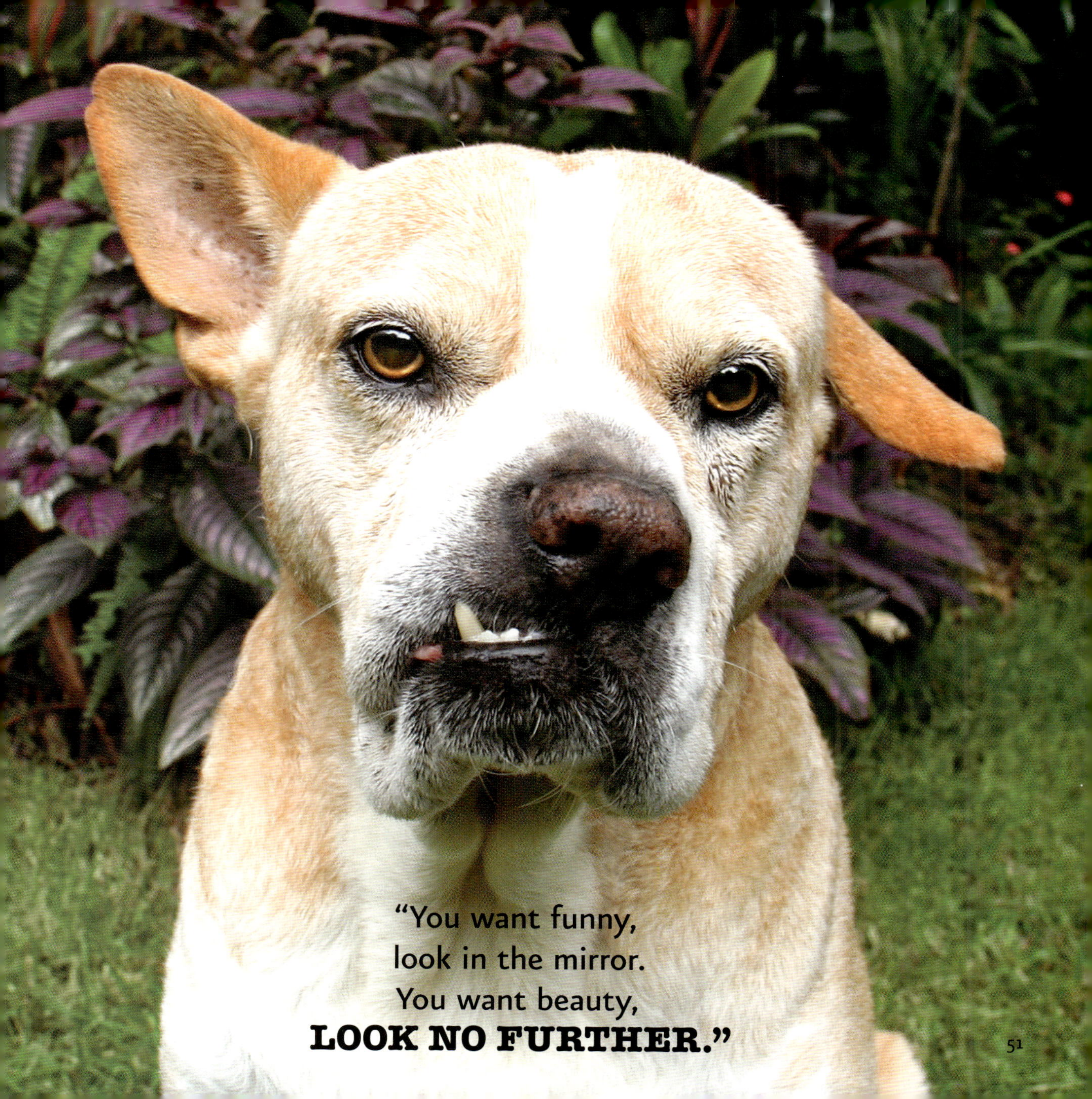

"You want funny,
look in the mirror.
You want beauty,
LOOK NO FURTHER."

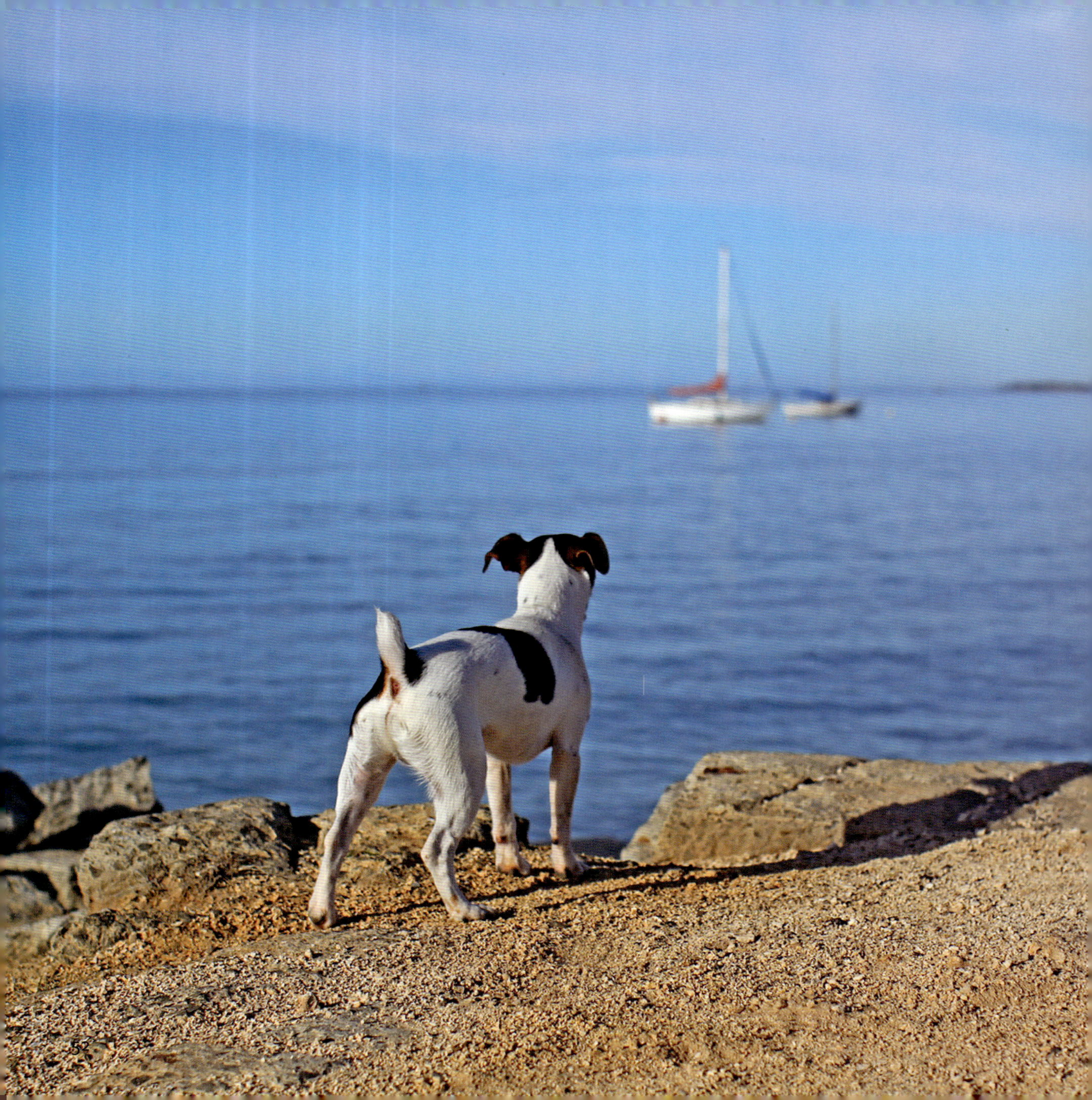

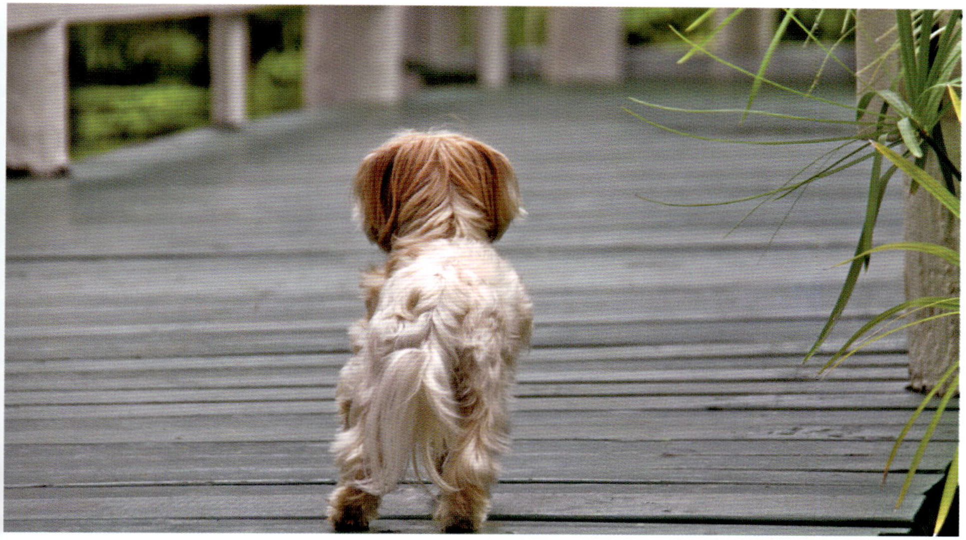

Tip: When your dog looks away at something interesting, step back and snap the photo. The result is a story, not just a picture.

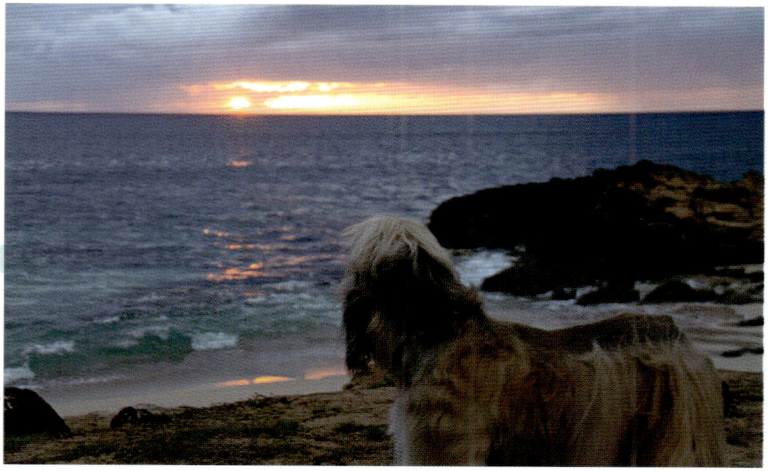

If you love a ball,
SET IT FREE.
If it comes back,
IT'S YOURS.
If it doesn't, then chances are some other dog ripped you off.
So, maybe you should just hold onto your... well, you know.

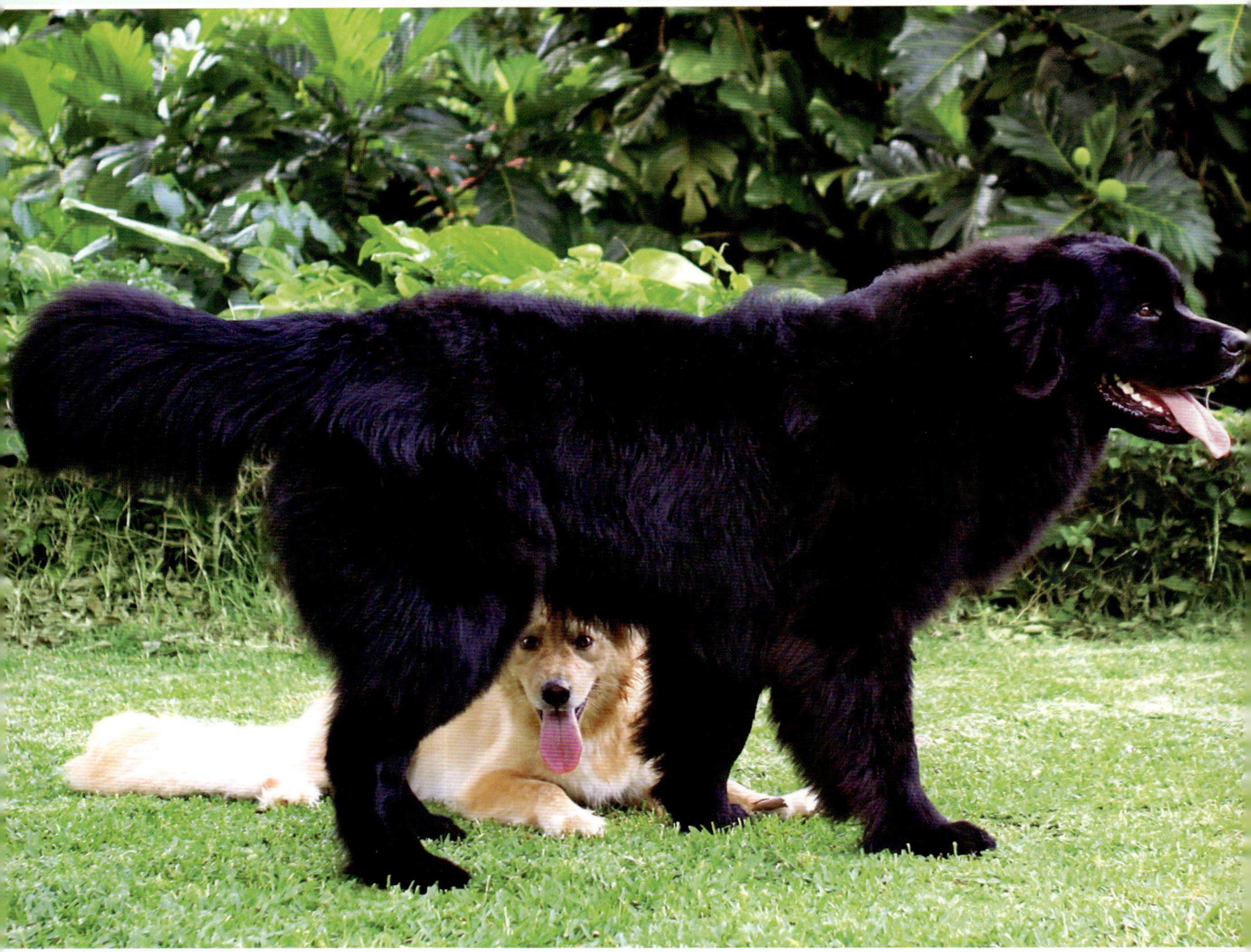

"In the theater we call this being
'UPSTAGED.'"

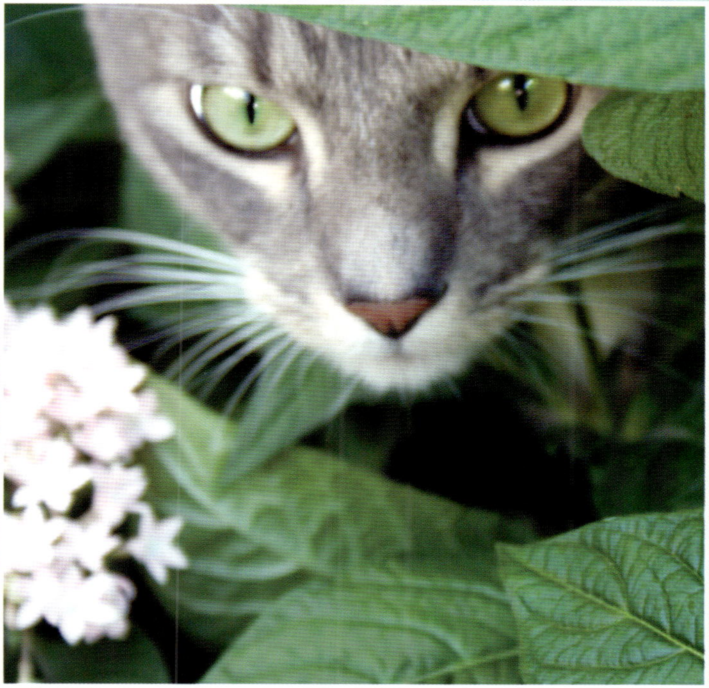

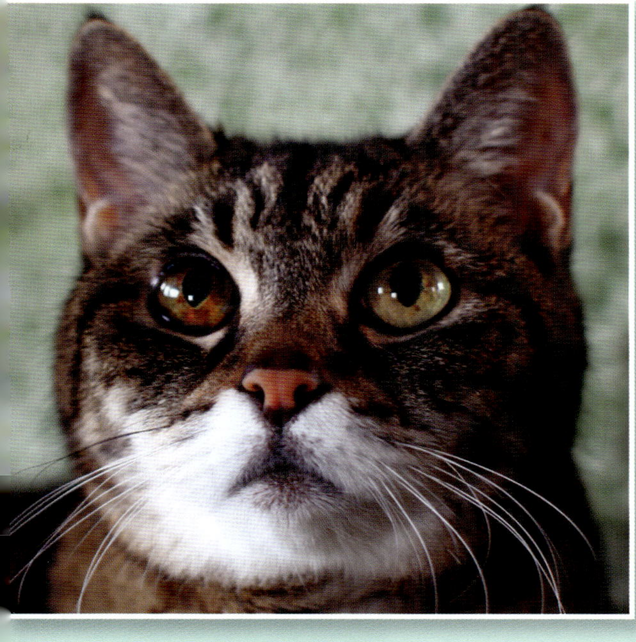

"PEEK-A-BOO!"

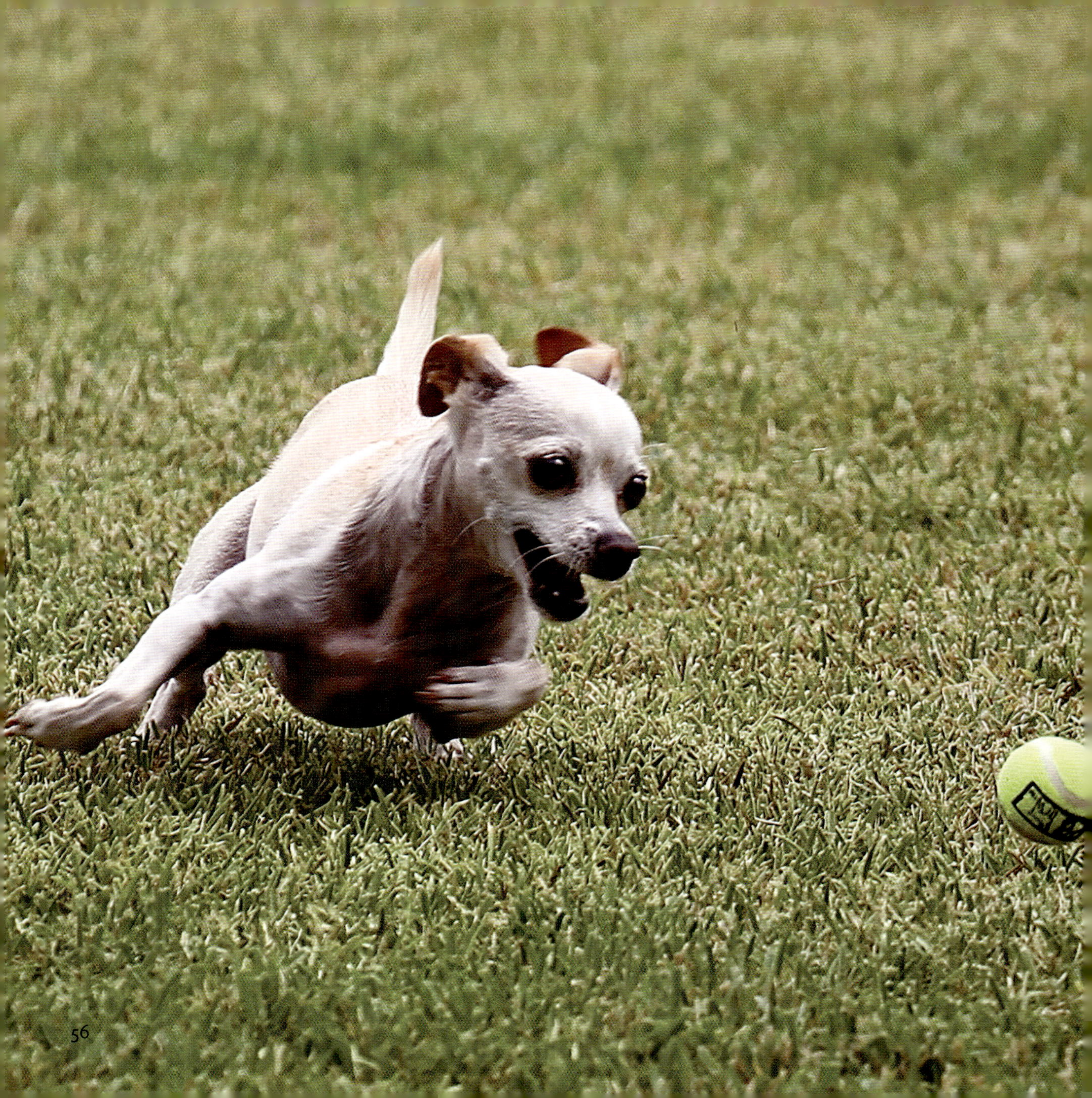

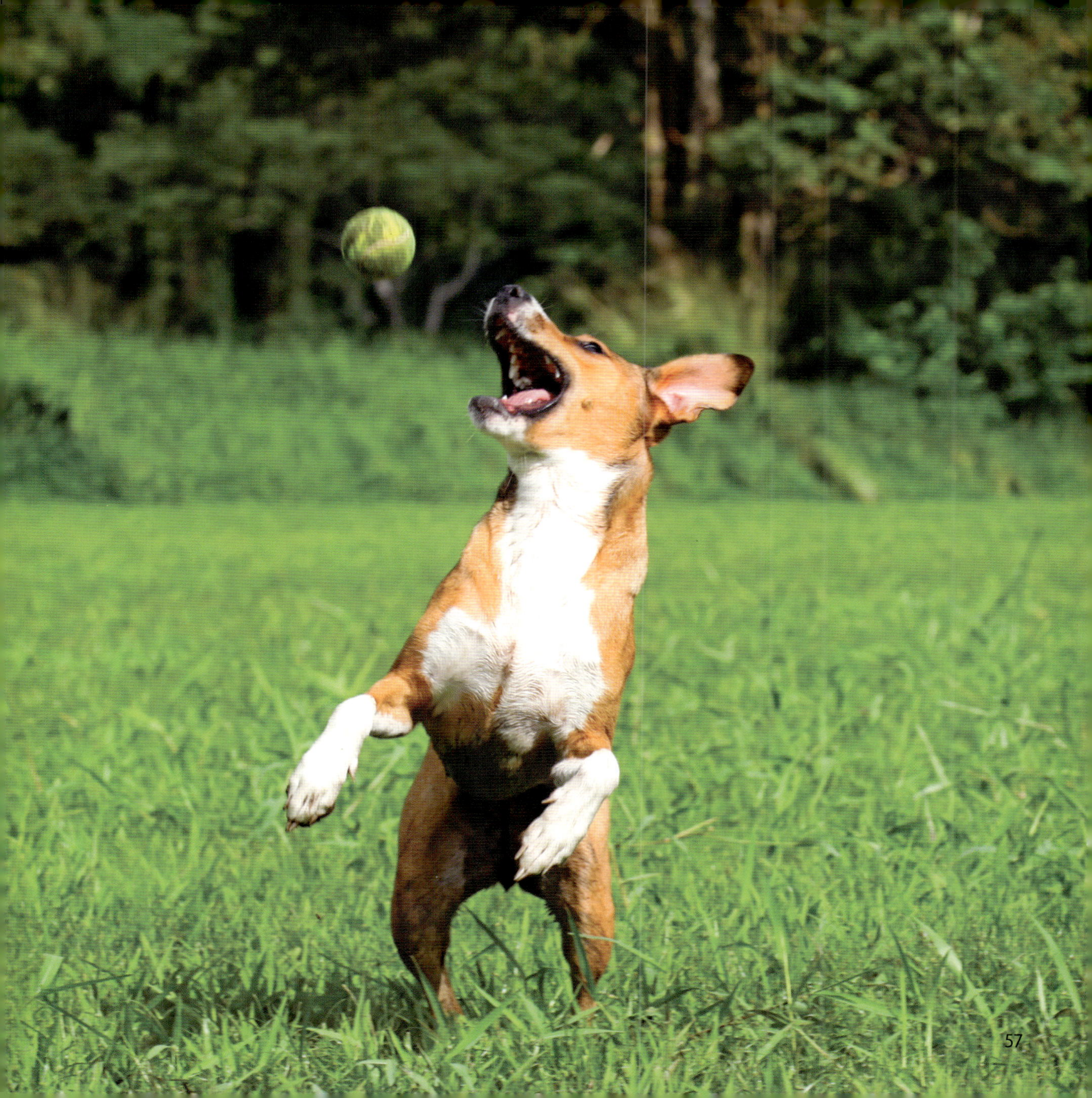

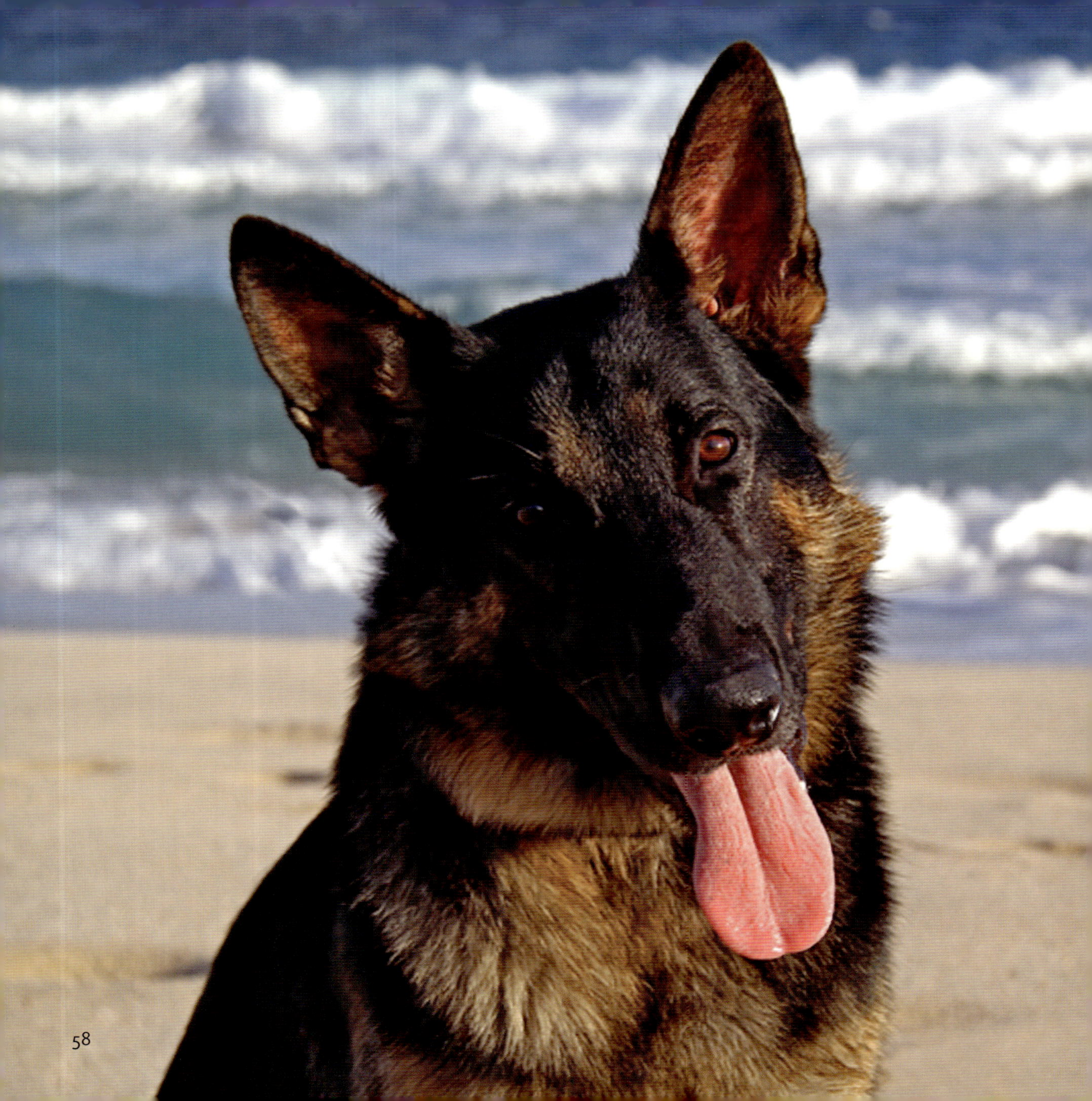

"Look into our eyes... you're getting sleepy... very, very sleepy... **NOW GO GET US A TREAT!"**

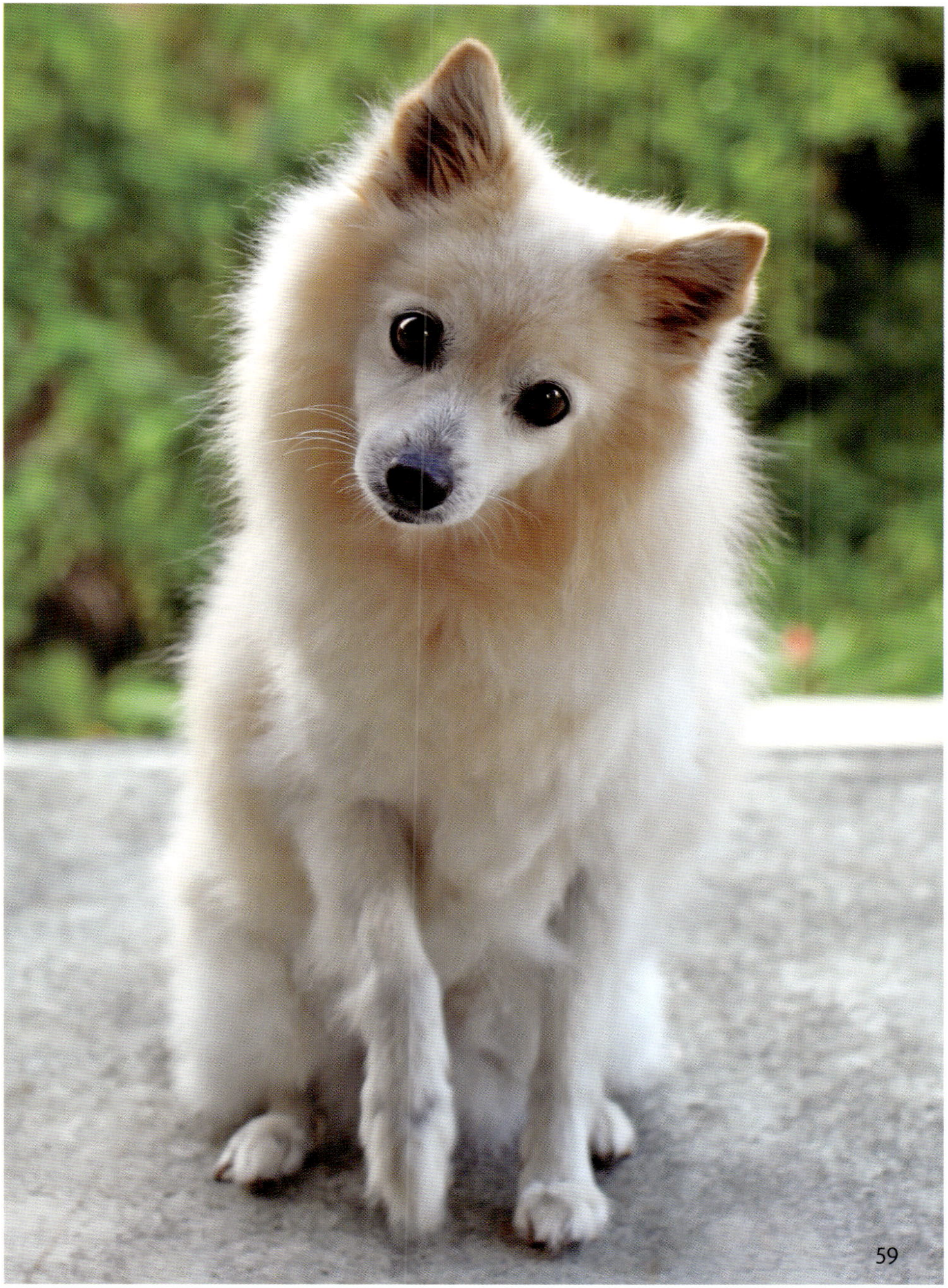

Tip: Get down at your pet's level, if not lower.

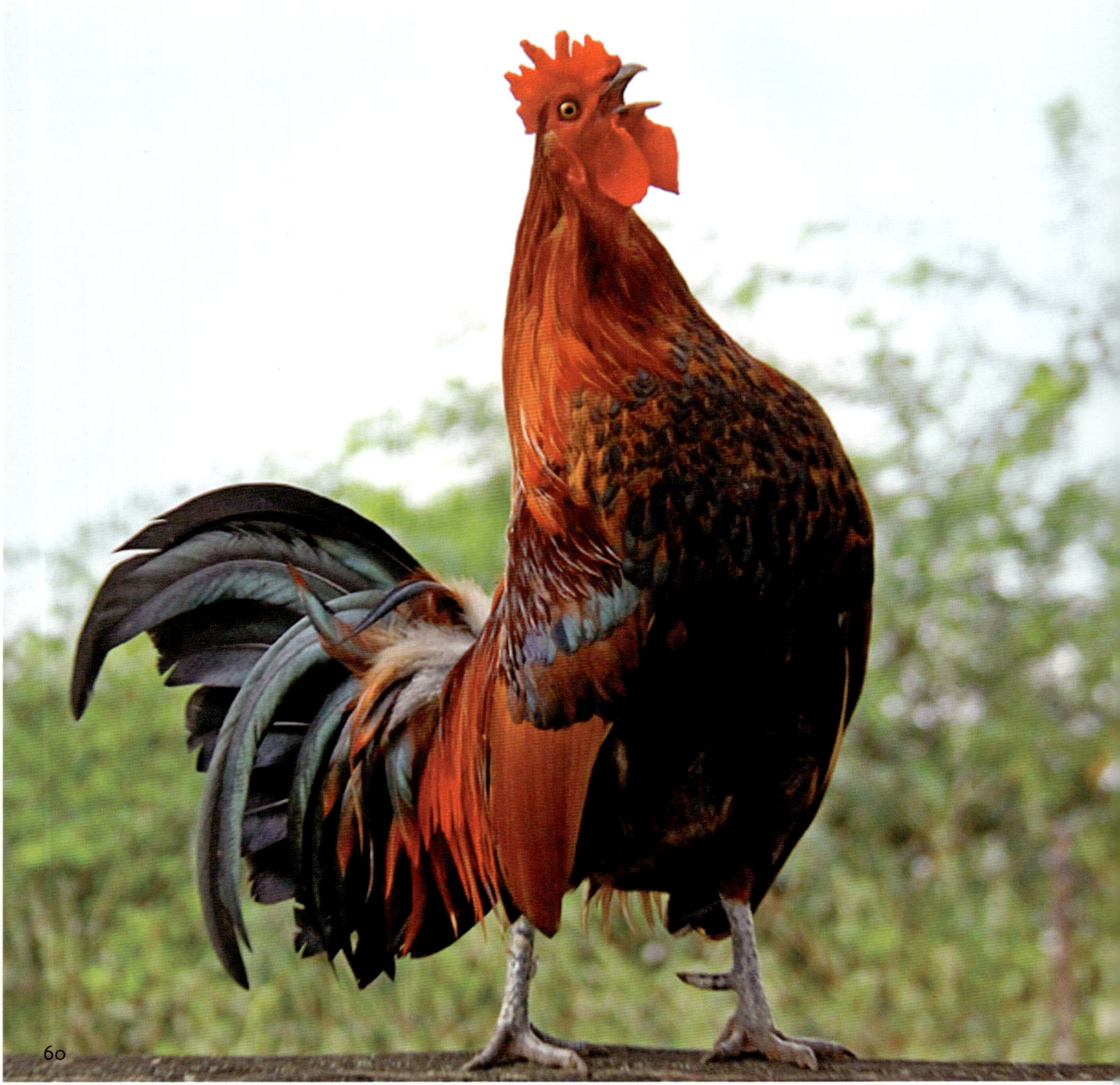

Hen talking:

"LOOK AT HIM!

Chest puffed, feathers out, and crowing like he did all the work.

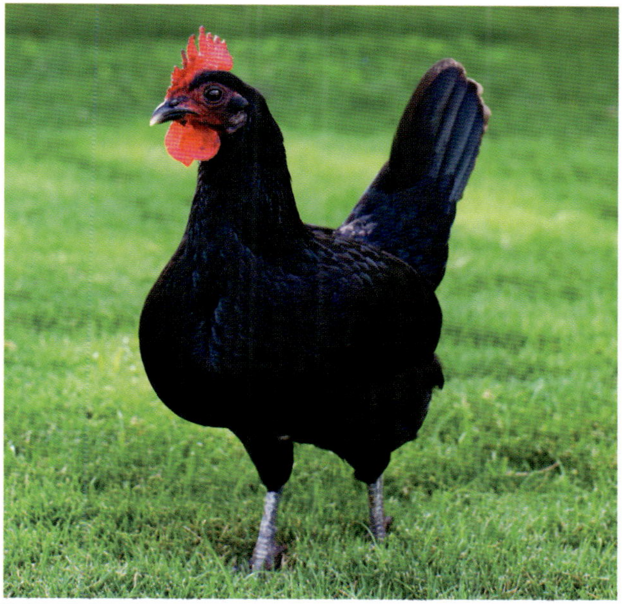

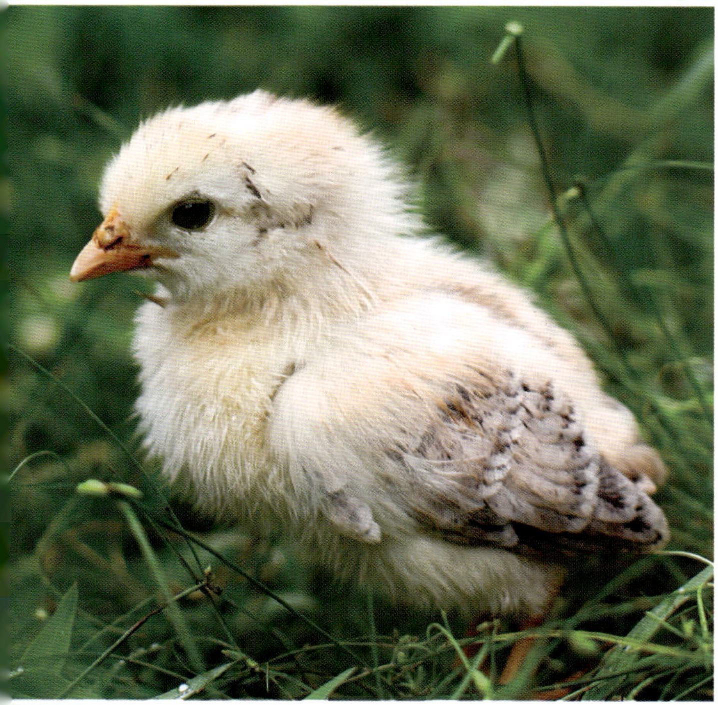

His effort, maybe two seconds. I have to pass an egg, sit on it and then hope I'm off before I catch a beak in the backside!"

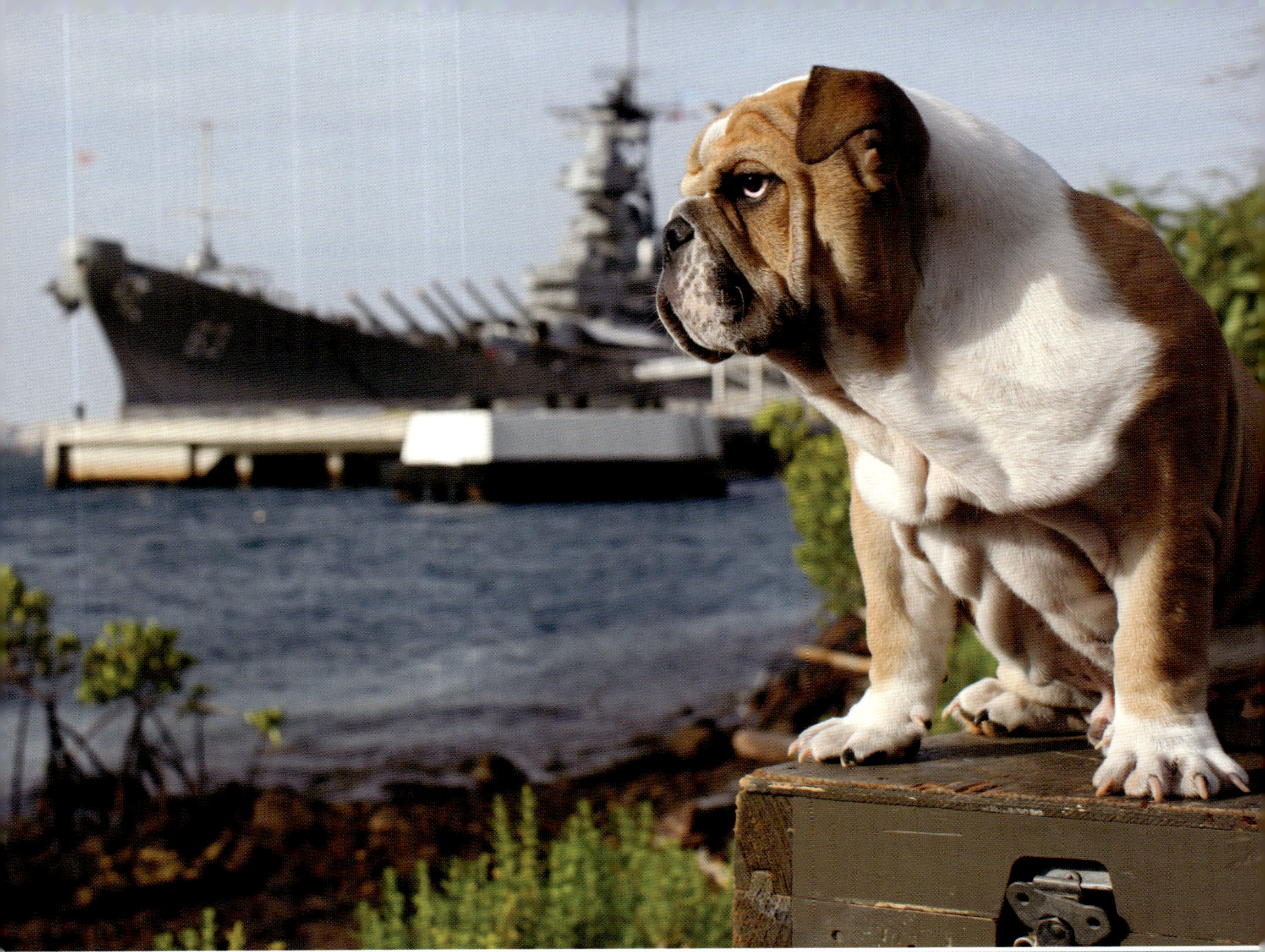

We celebrate the
STRENGTH at the end.

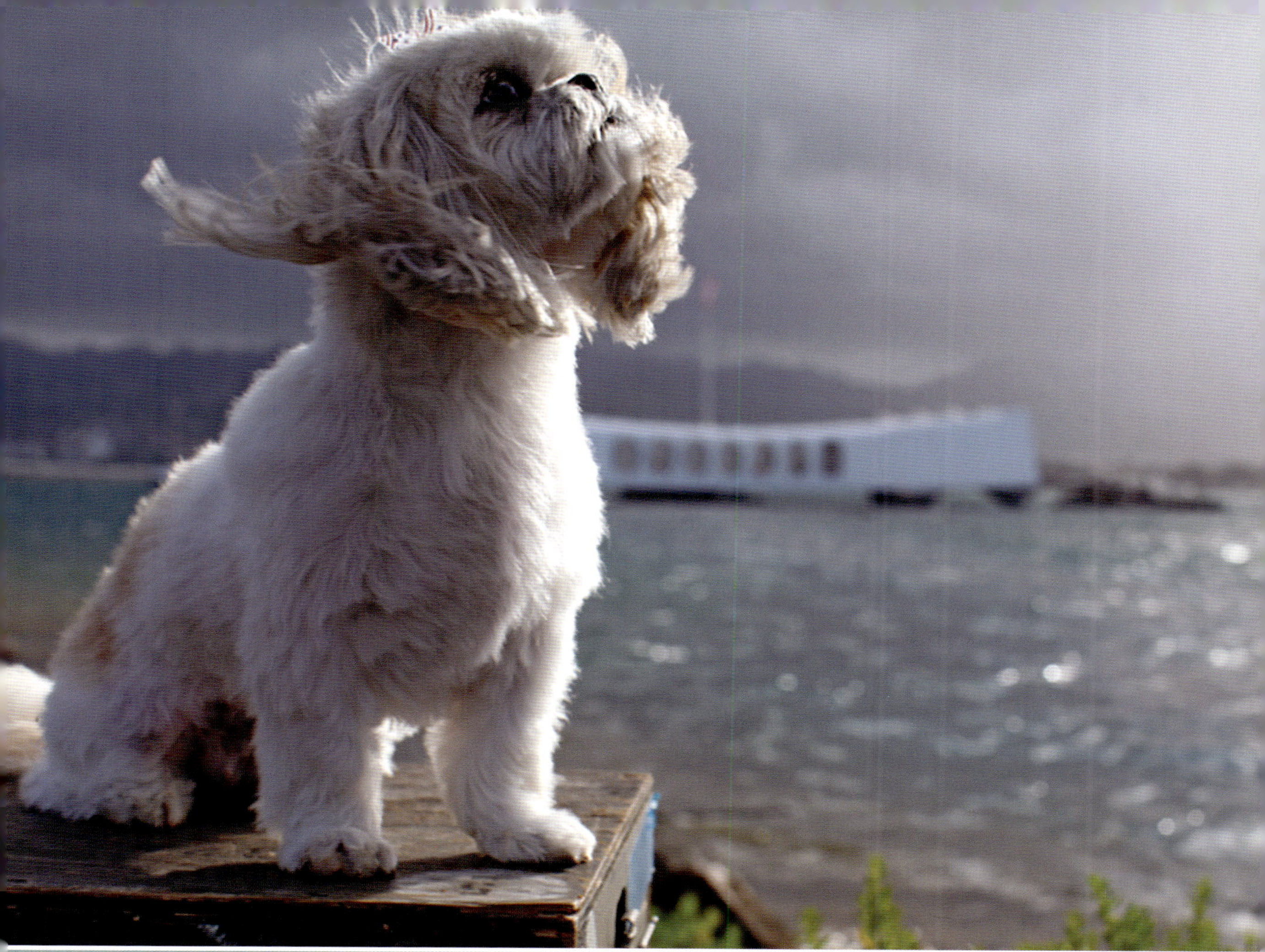

We contemplate the **SACRIFICE**
that was the beginning.

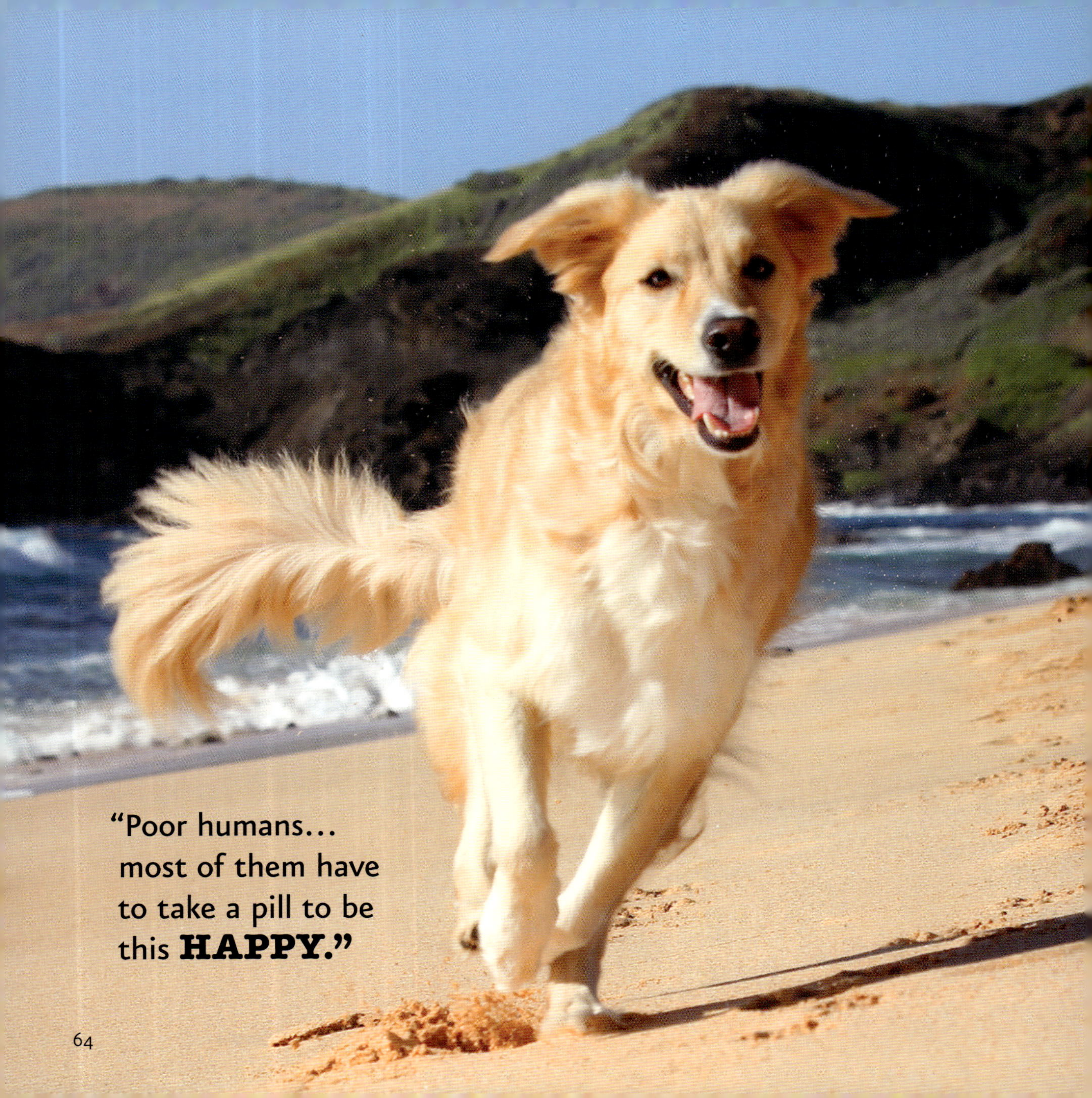

"Poor humans…
most of them have
to take a pill to be
this **HAPPY.**"

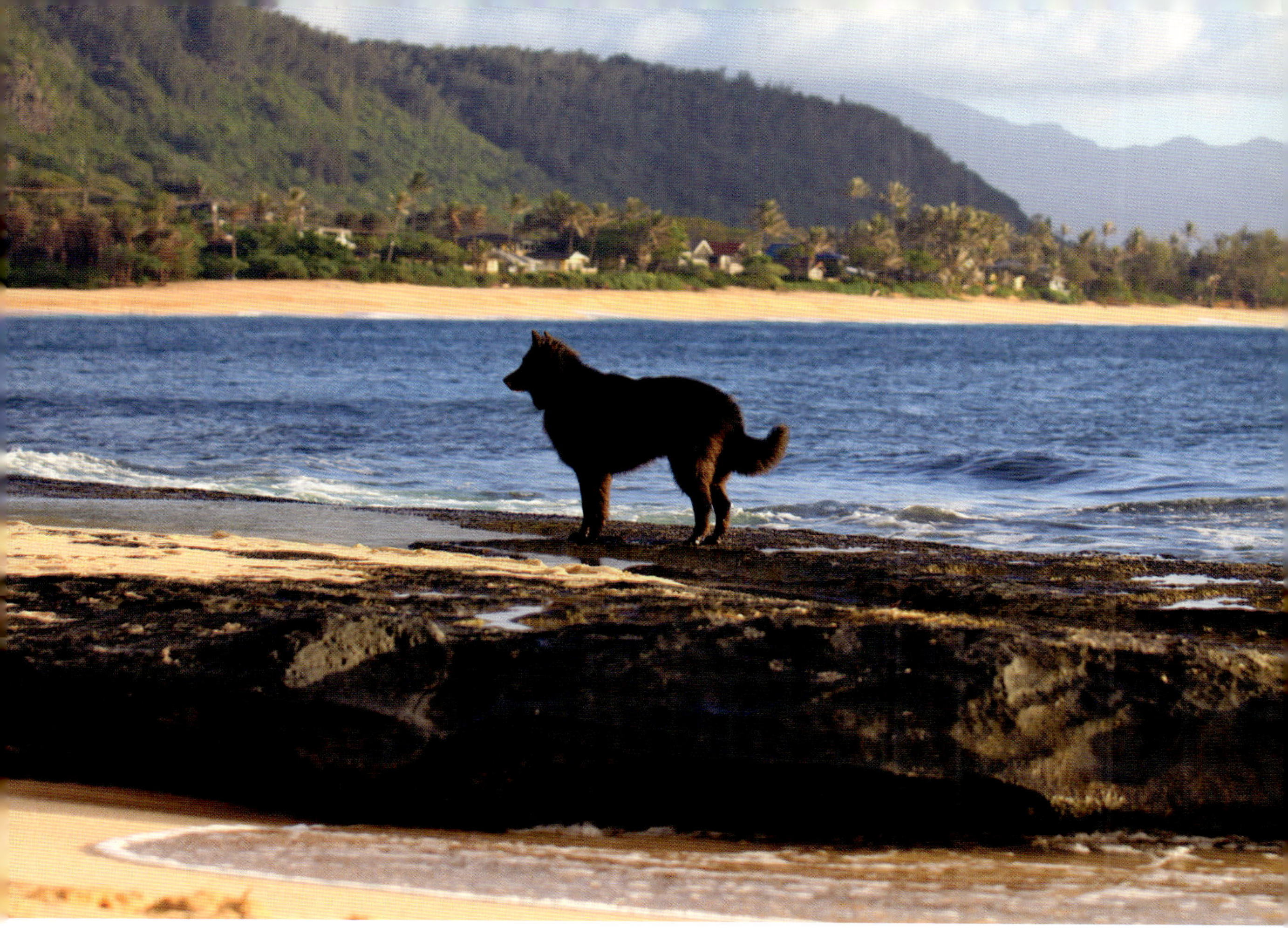

Just another day in
PARADISE.

Tip: Change in proximity to your subject can change the composition and end result completely.

HOW TO RESCUE A

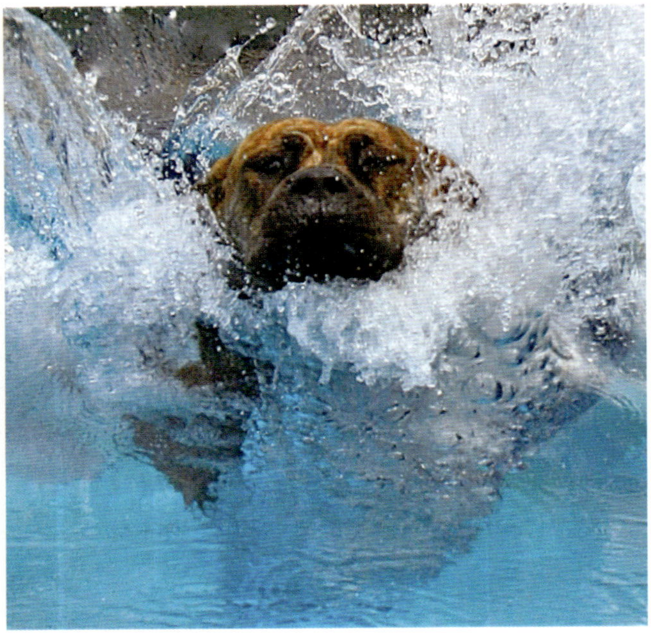

1. Enter water with head up.

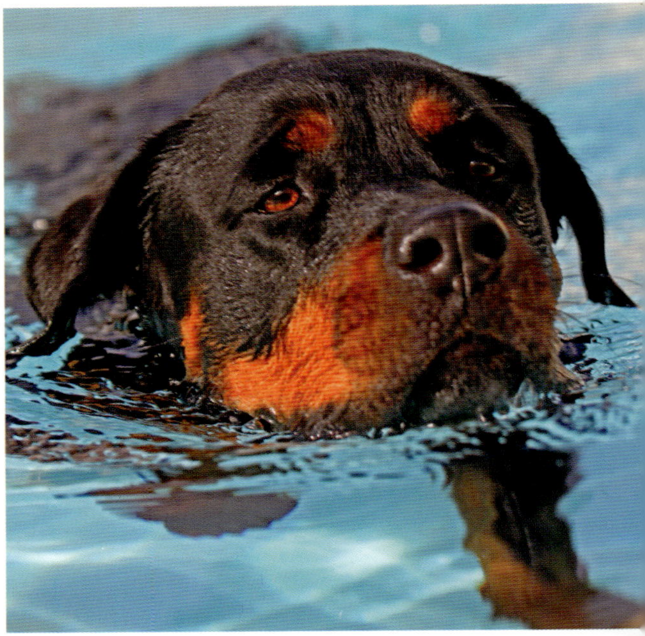

2. Swim.

DROWNING TENNIS BALL:

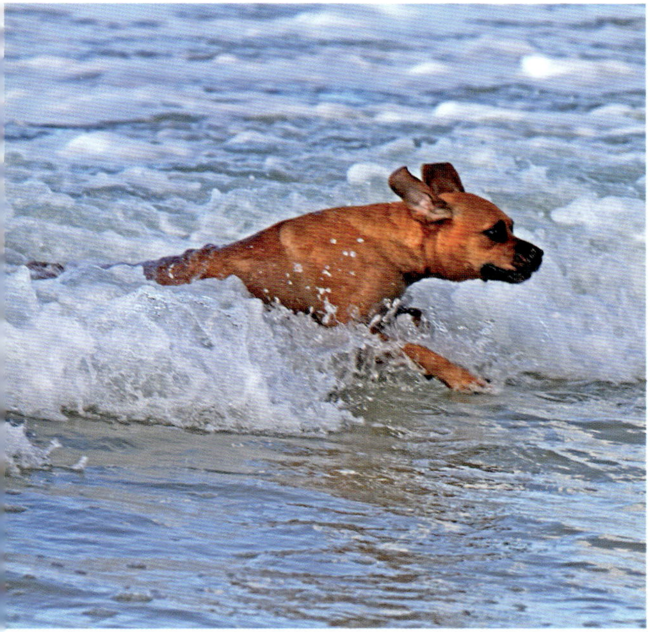

3. Swim harder.

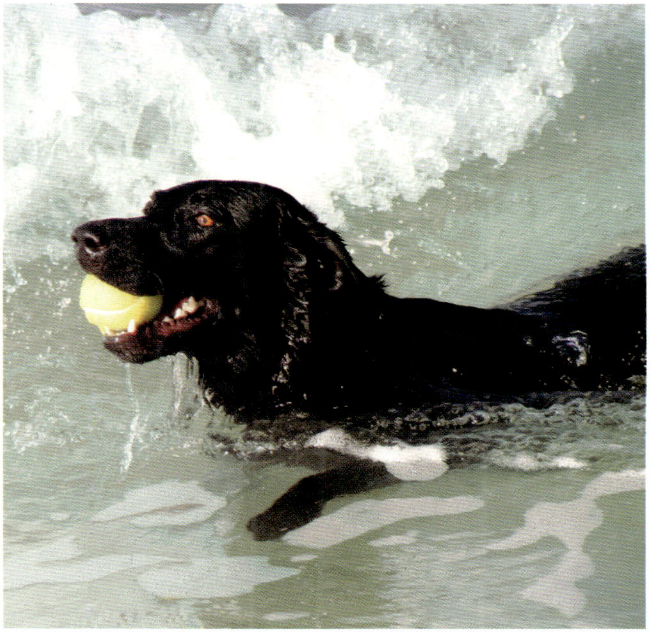

4. Retrieve drowning ball and return to shore.

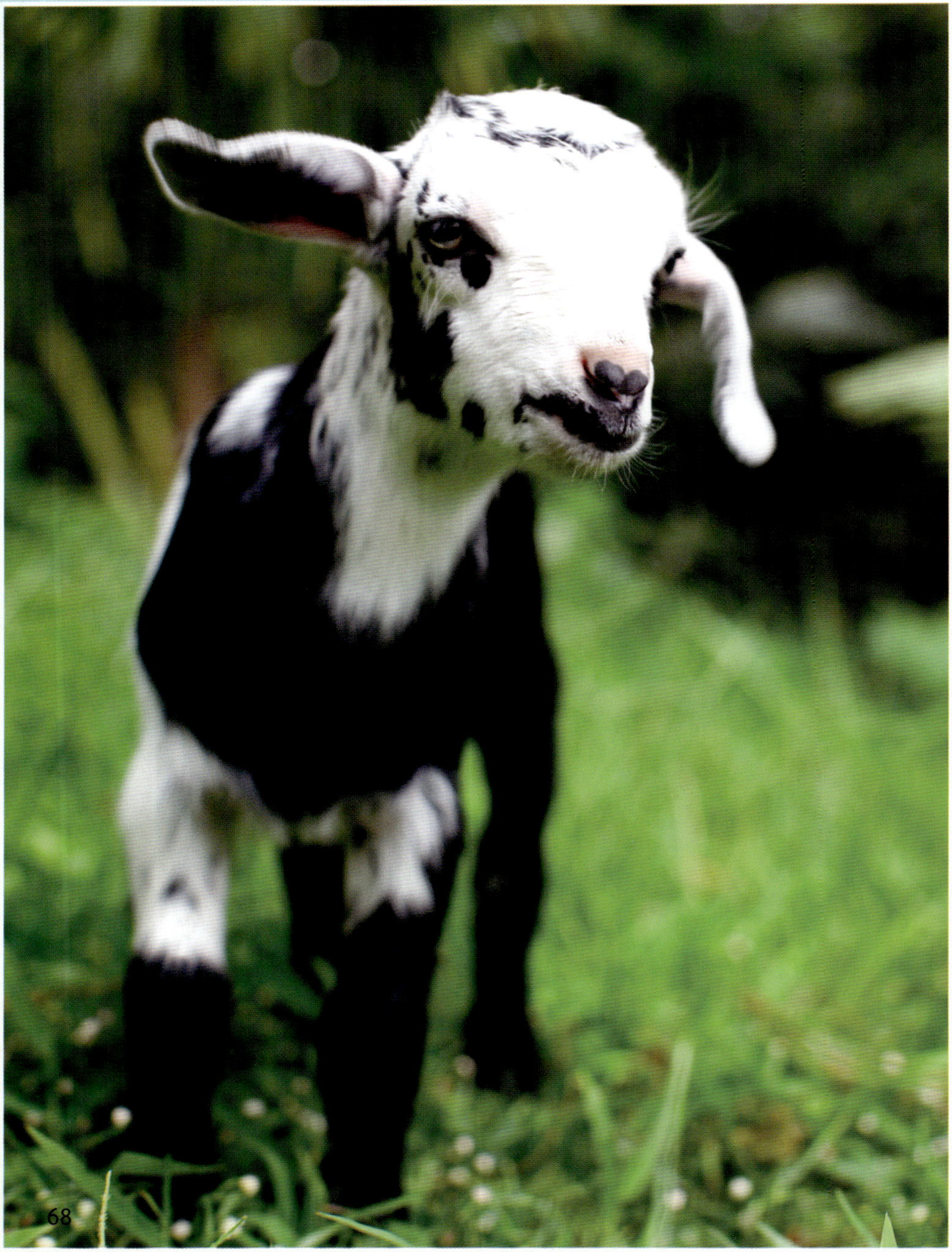

"DADDY!"

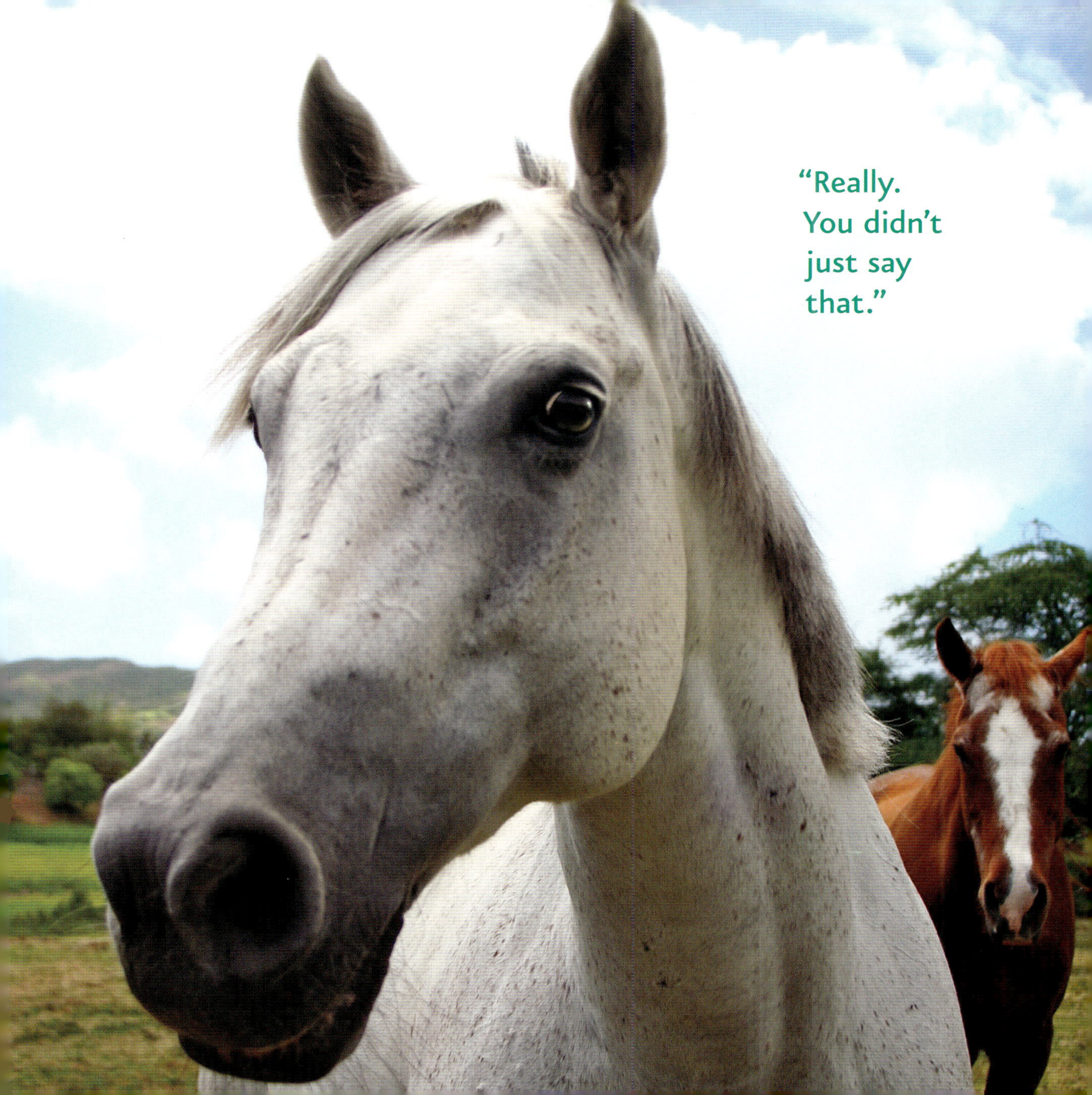

"Really.
You didn't
just say
that."

The newest craze sweeping Hawai‘i… **POTBELLY PIG SURFING…** not sure those qualify as toes hanging over though.

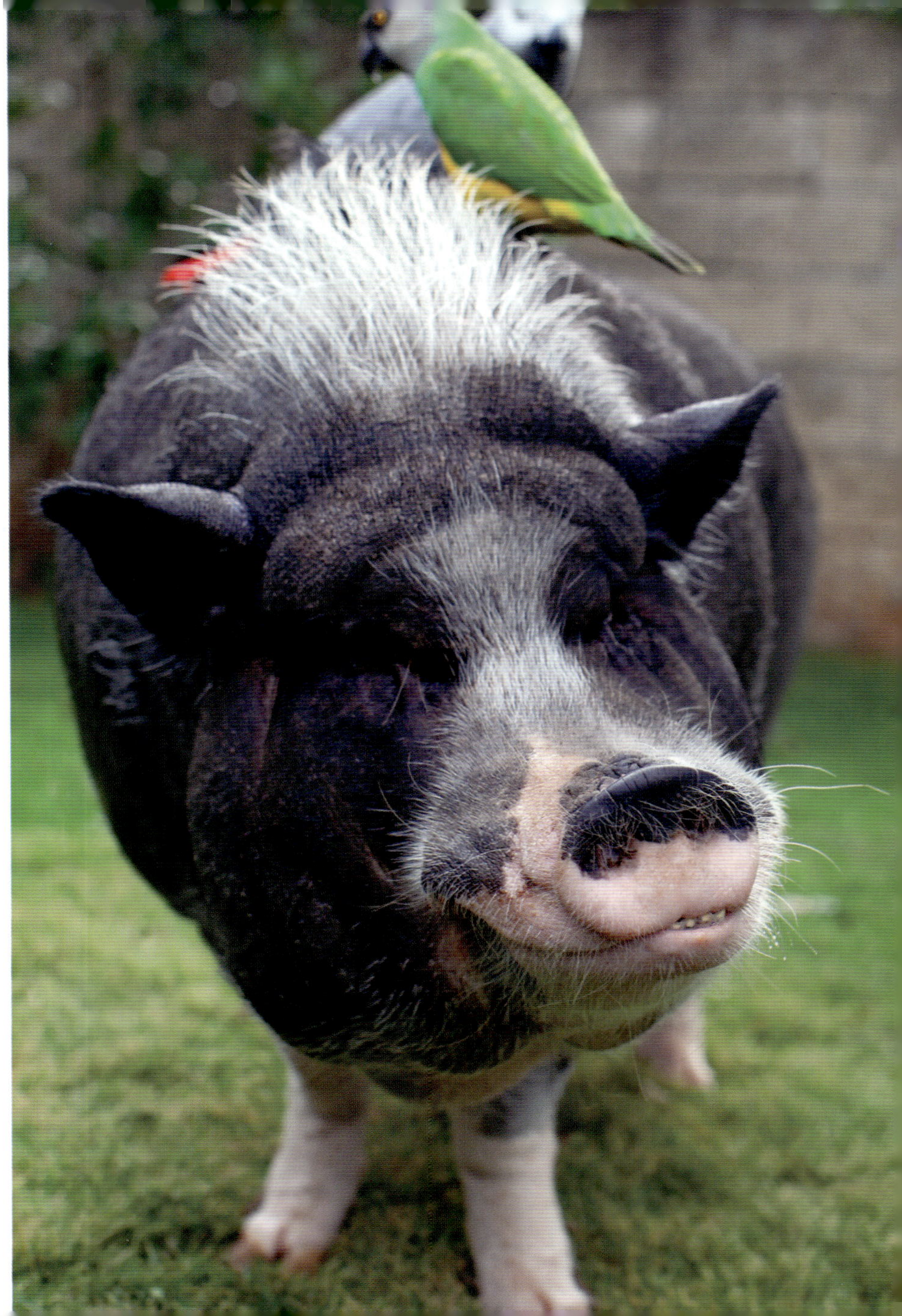

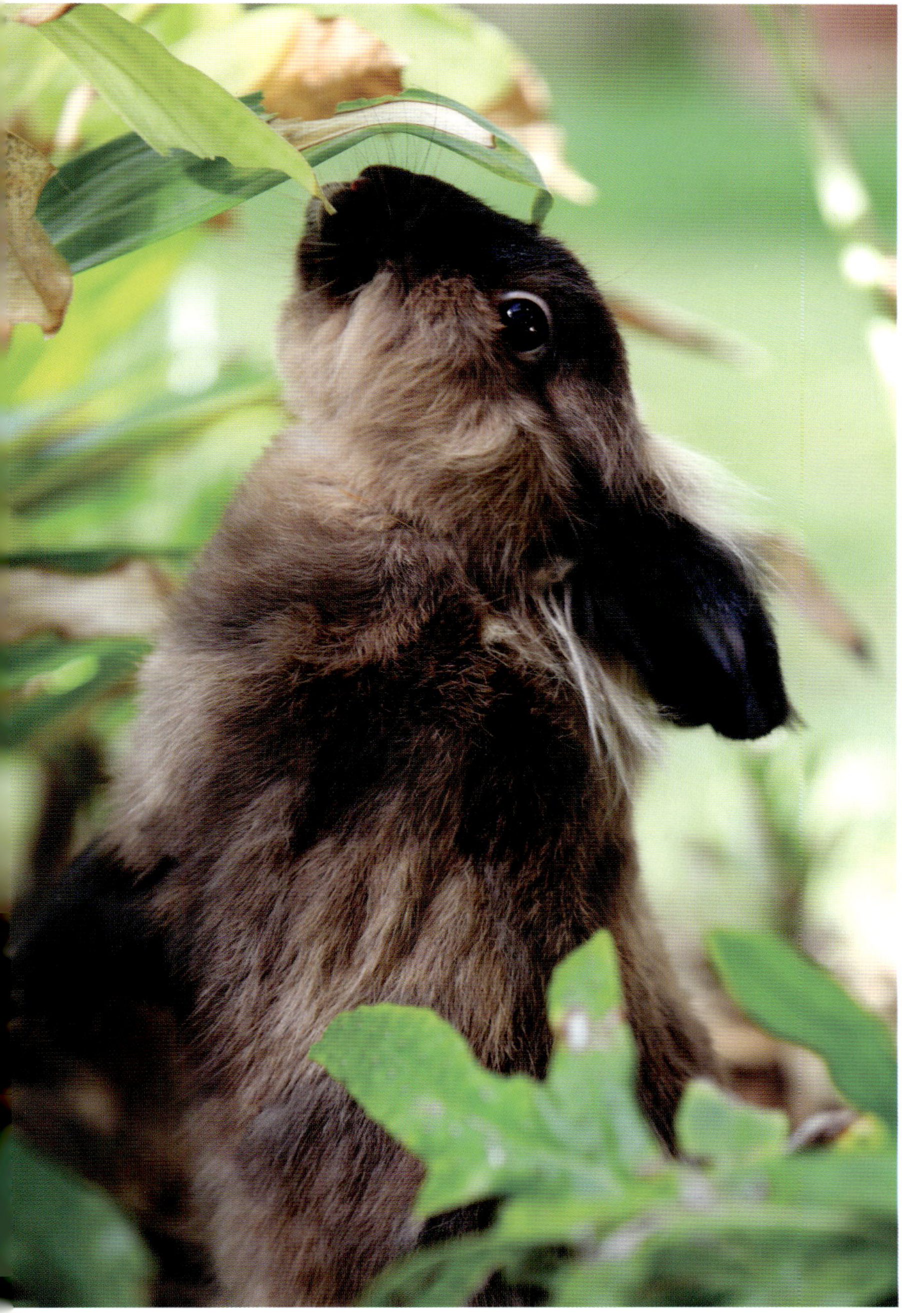

"Whoa! Did I just see two birds riding on a **PIG?!** I gotta lay off this **GREEN STUFF.**"

Tip: Much like a teenager's phone, a pet parent's camera should be permanently attached. You never know when your pet will do something fabulous.

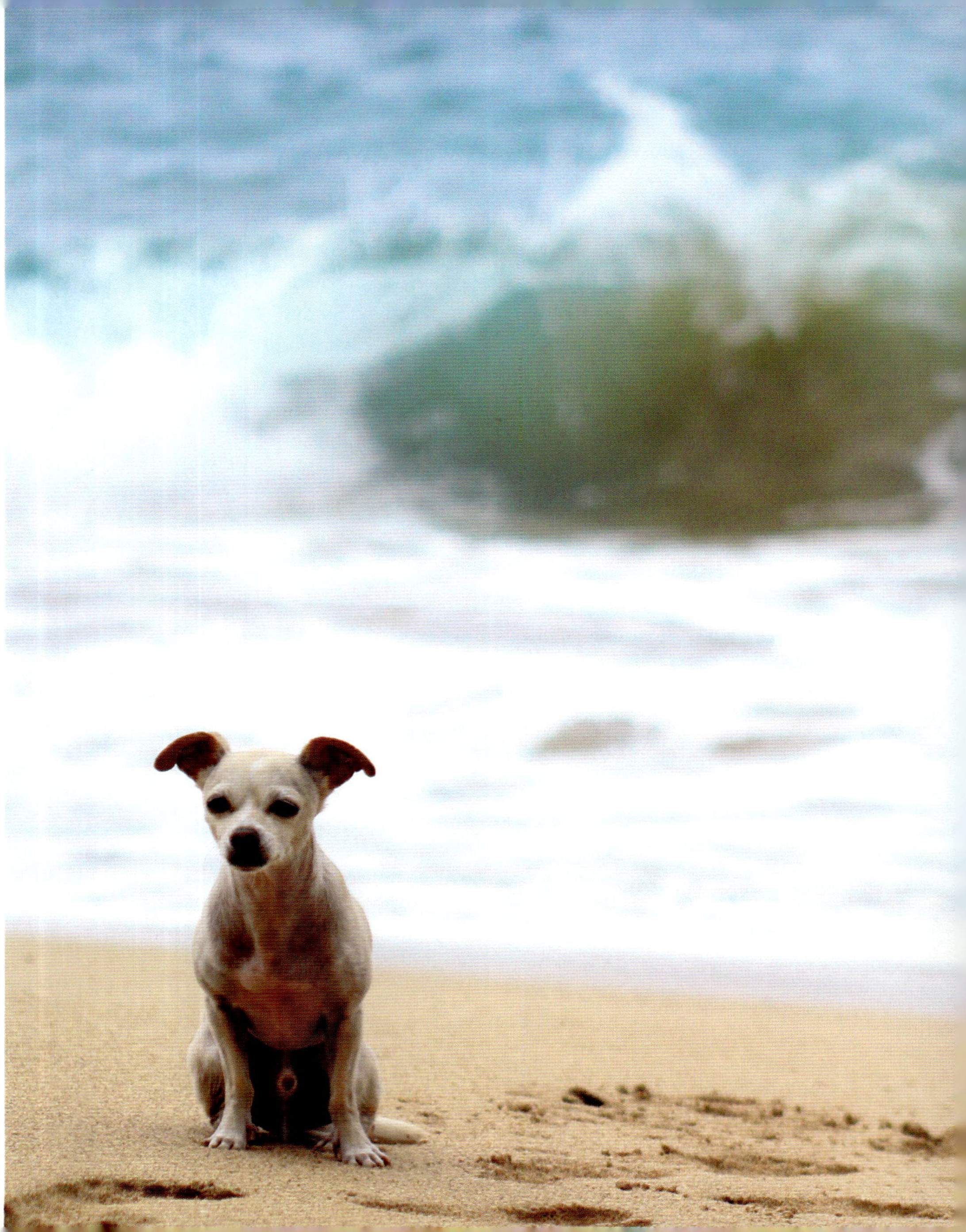

"OK, I'll stay, but if that wave takes me out you better be prepared to hand over a whole **LOT** of doggie treats."

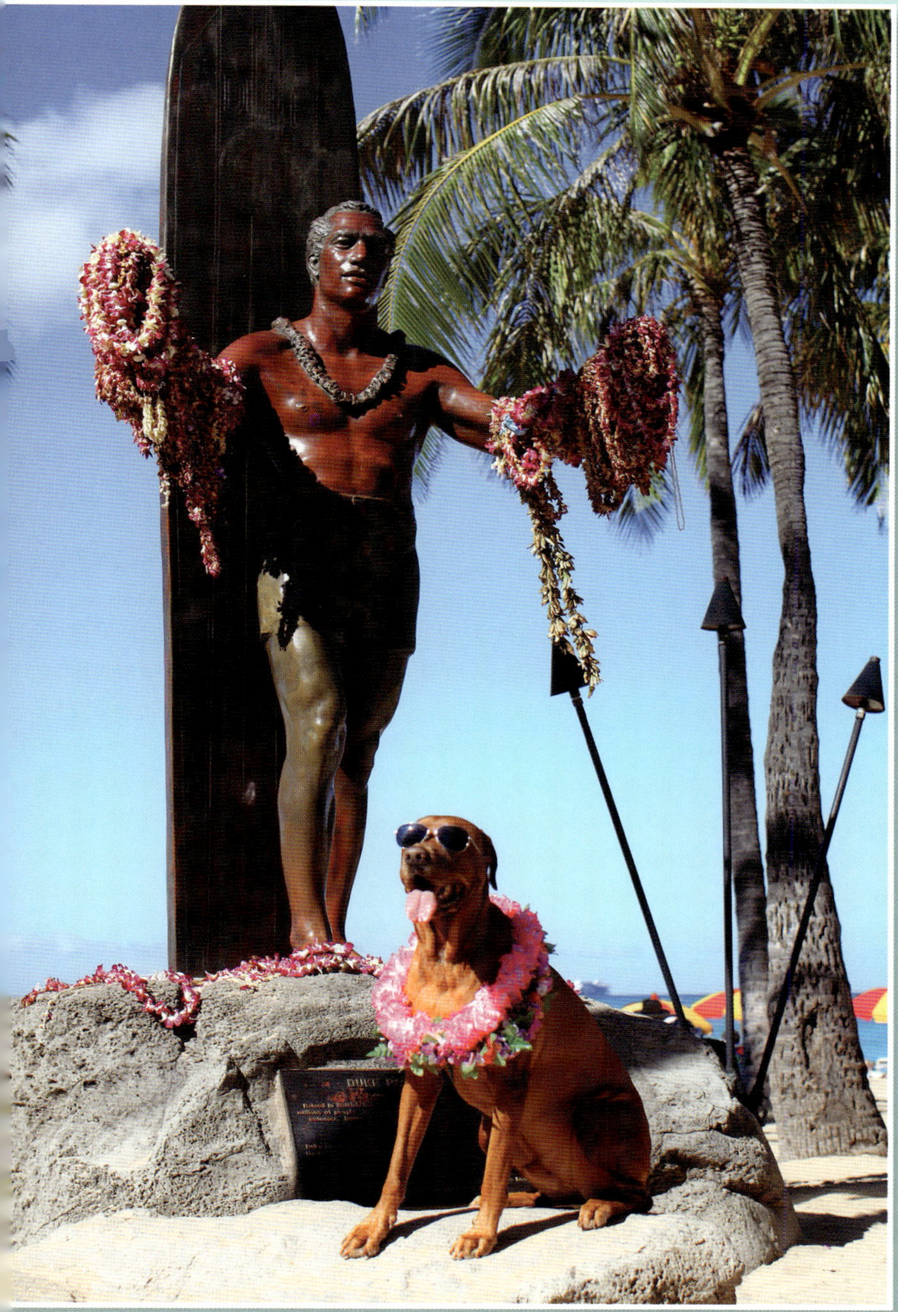

"CHICKS DIG ME."

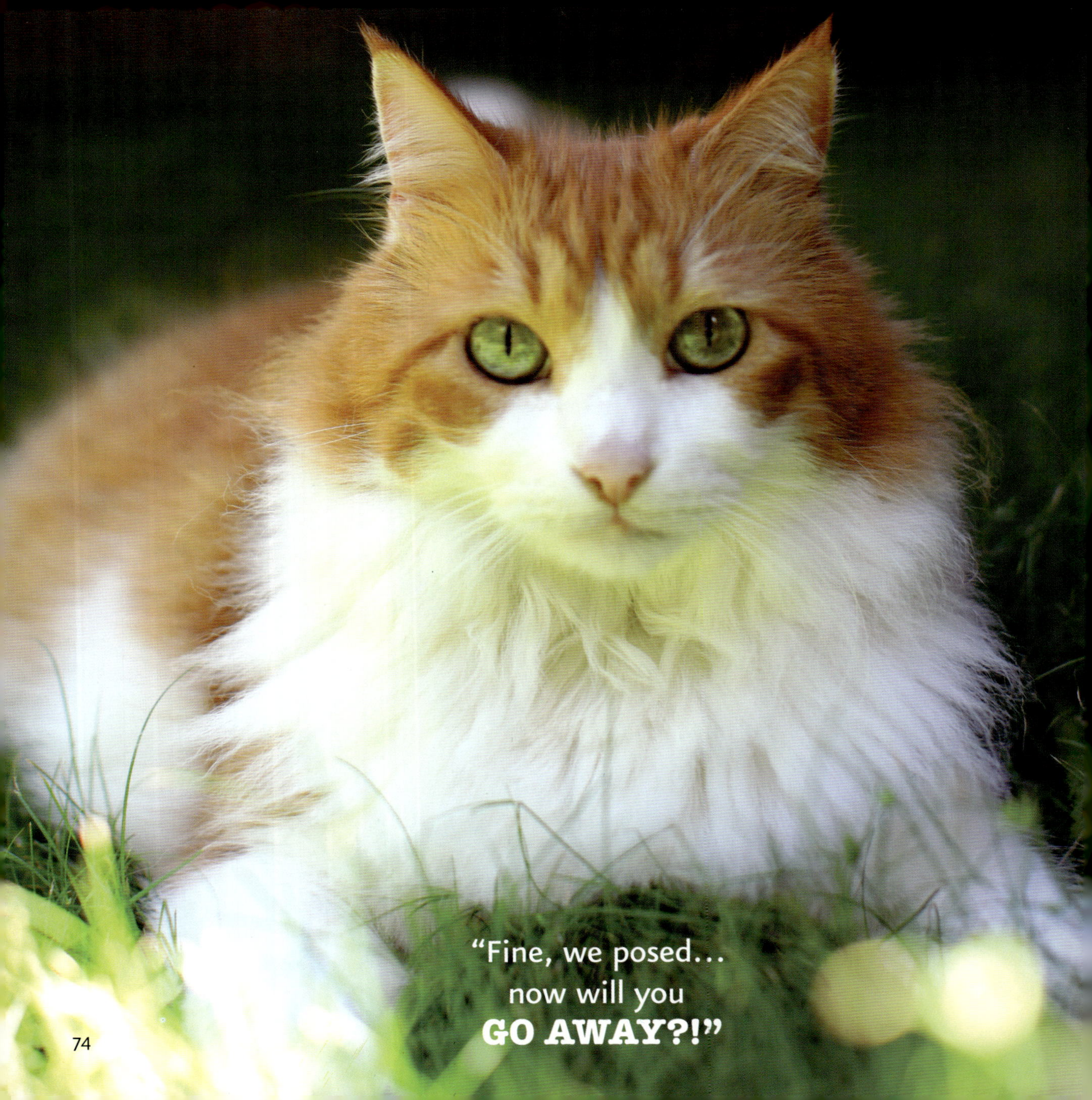

"Fine, we posed...
now will you
GO AWAY?!"

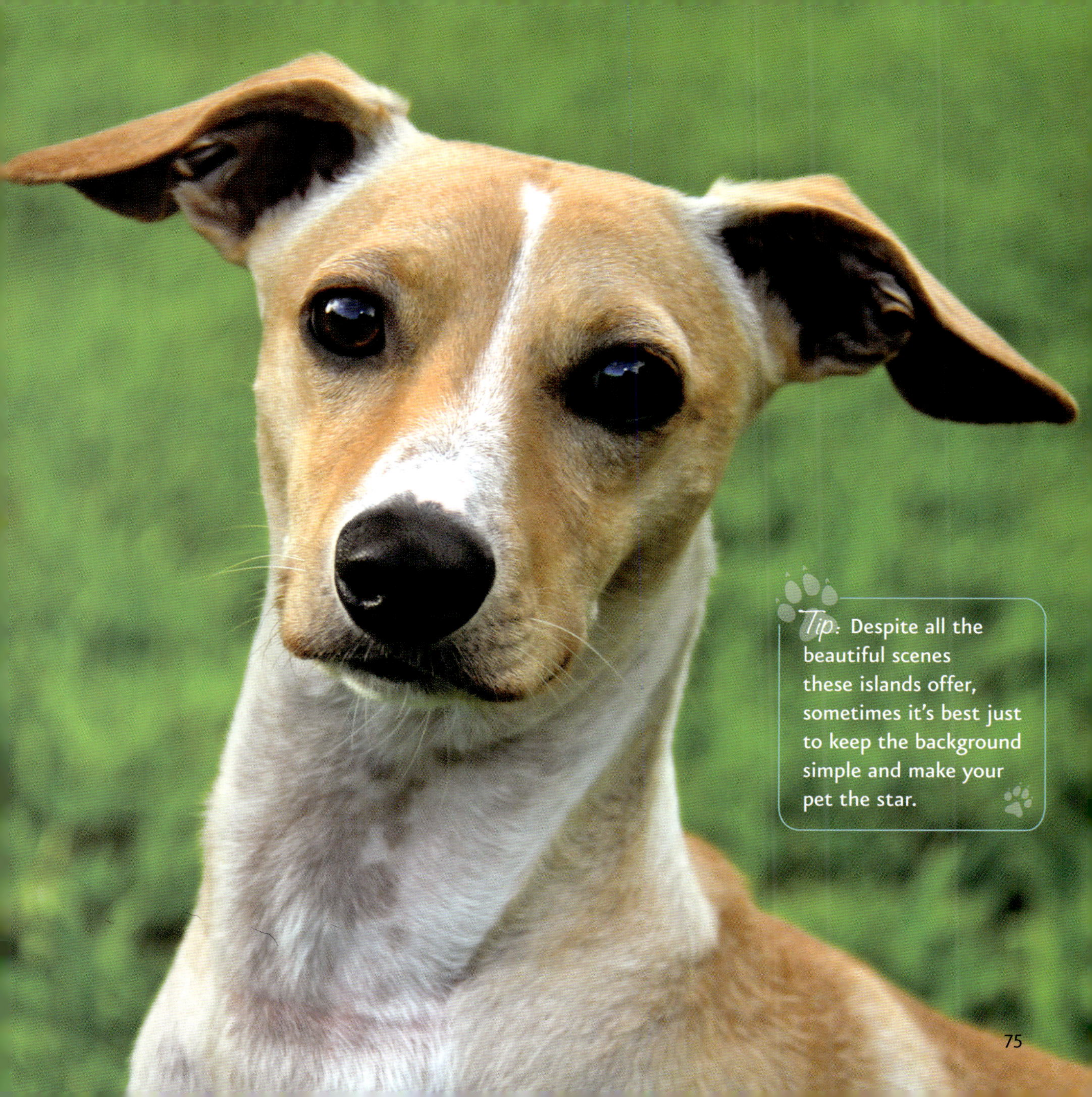

Tip: Despite all the beautiful scenes these islands offer, sometimes it's best just to keep the background simple and make your pet the star.

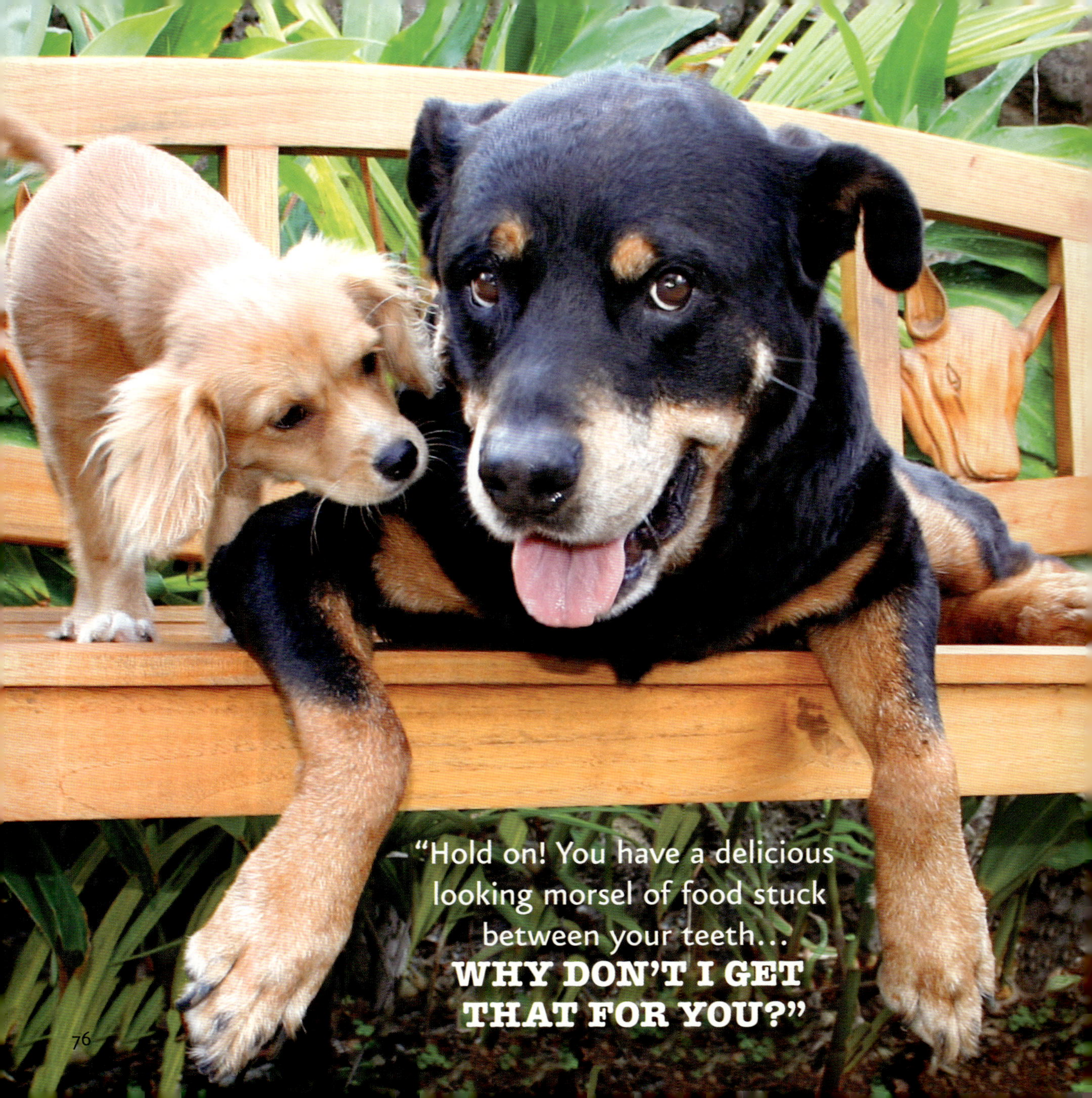

“Hold on! You have a delicious looking morsel of food stuck between your teeth…
WHY DON’T I GET THAT FOR YOU?”

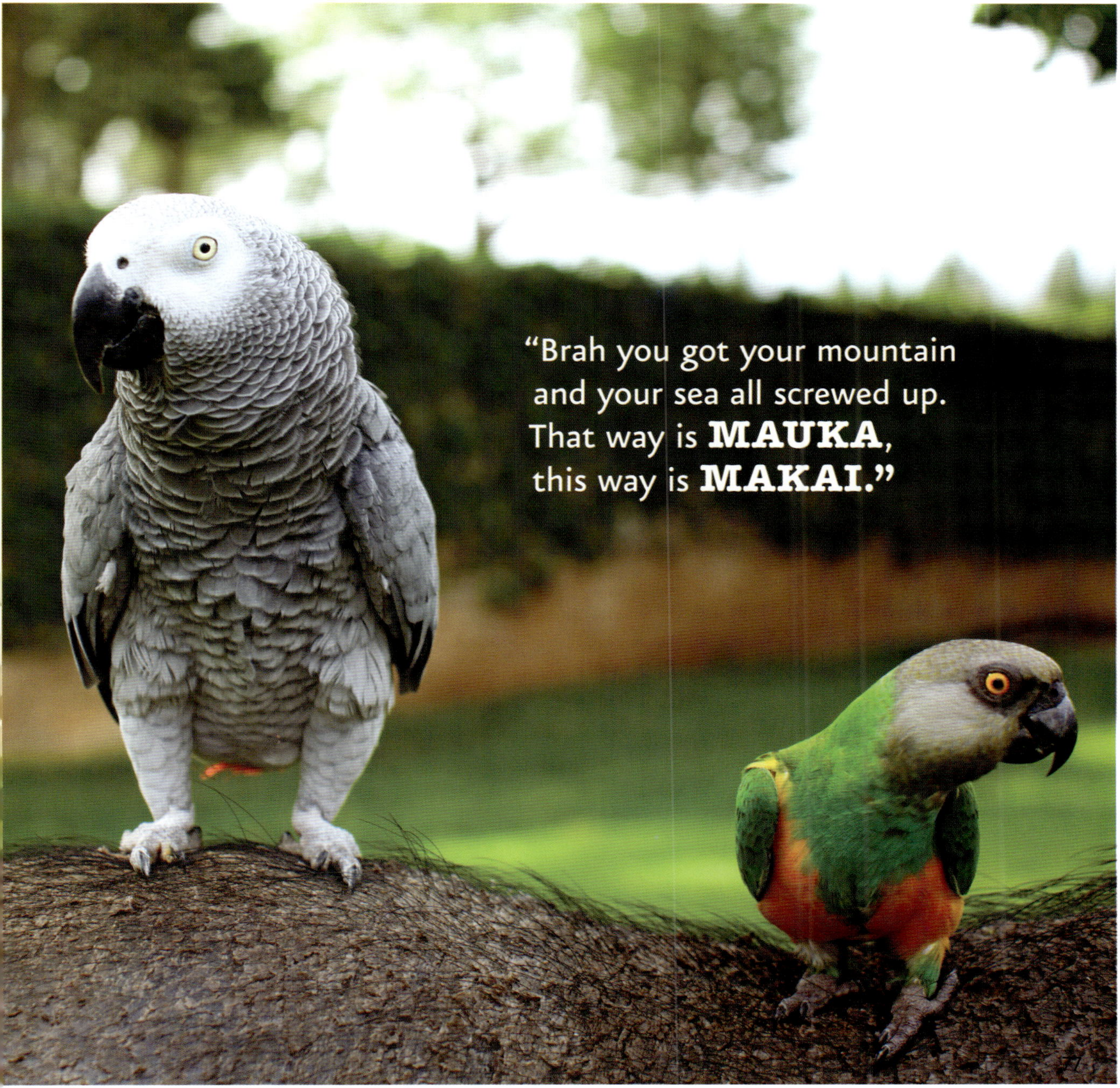

"Brah you got your mountain and your sea all screwed up. That way is **MAUKA**, this way is **MAKAI.**"

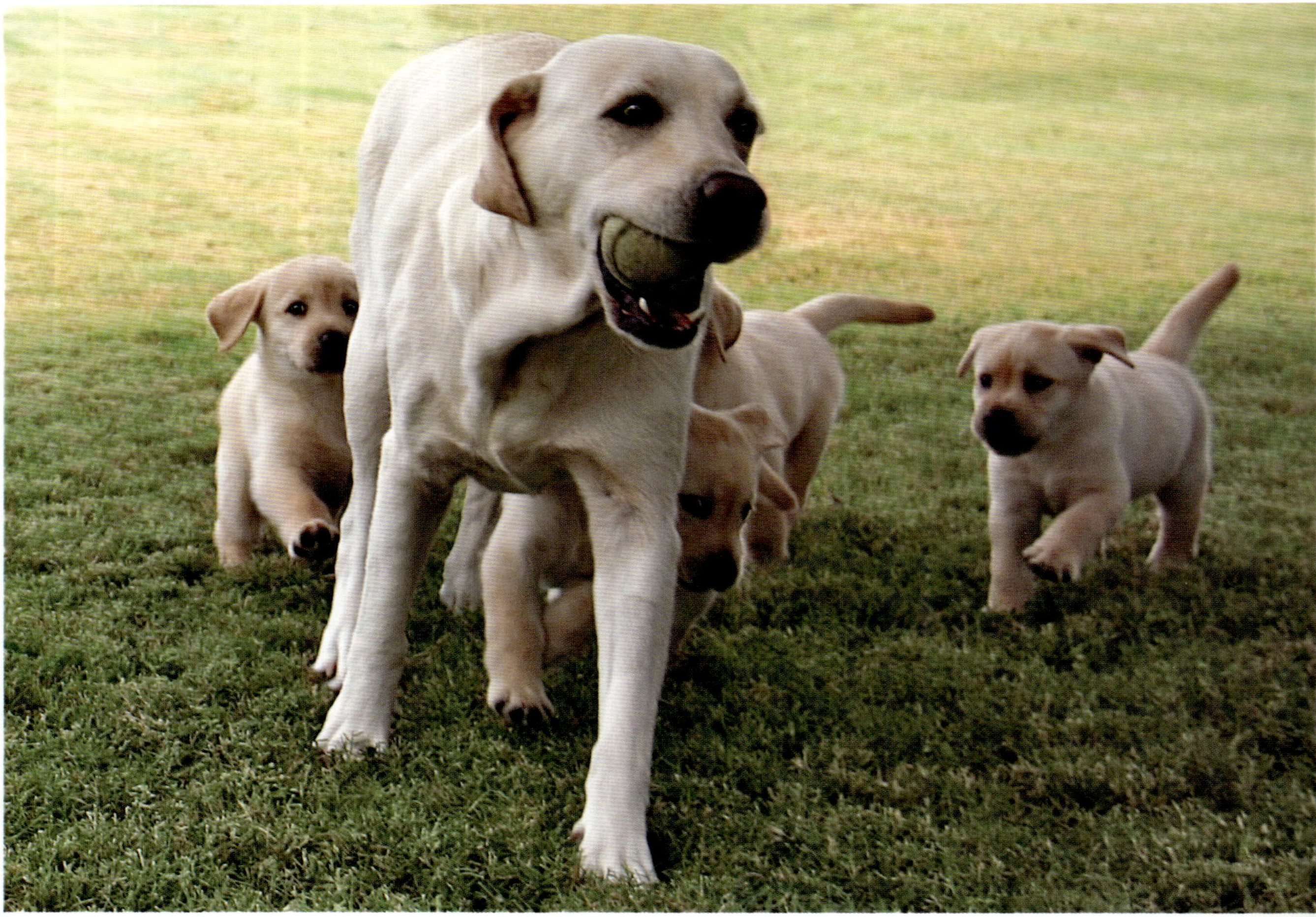

"If one more of you ankle biters yells **'MOMMY,'** I'm gonna howl!"

Tip: Pet photography requires patience. Photographing puppies requires **PATIENCE**... yes, **PATIENCE** in big, bold capitals. If you are going to photograph a litter, make certain that you have plenty of help and that your help is forewarned to wear closed toe shoes to avoid puppy poop piles.

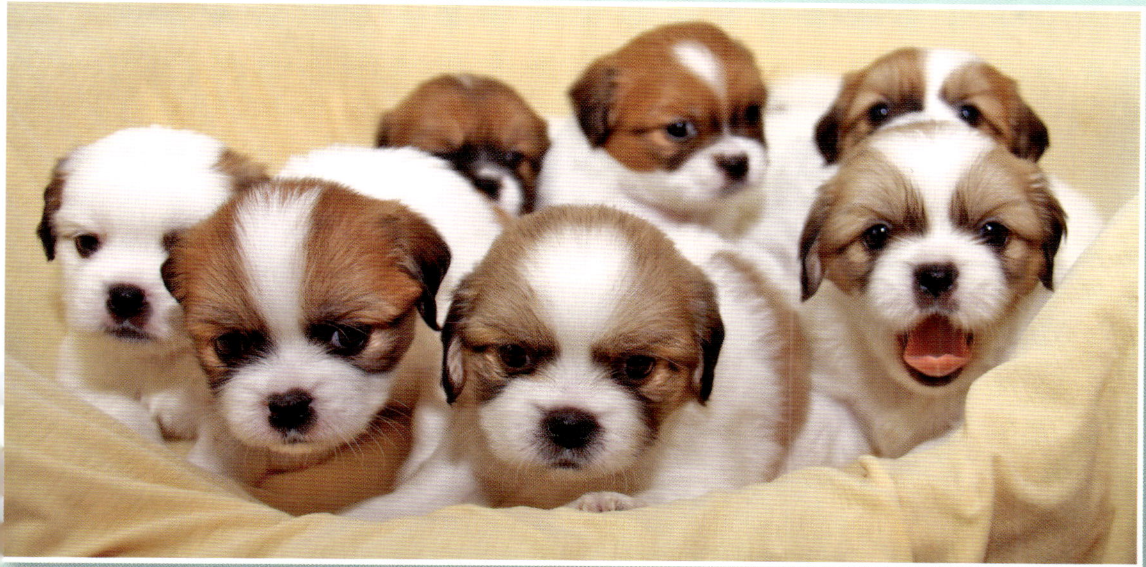

"Aww! Who wet the basket?!"

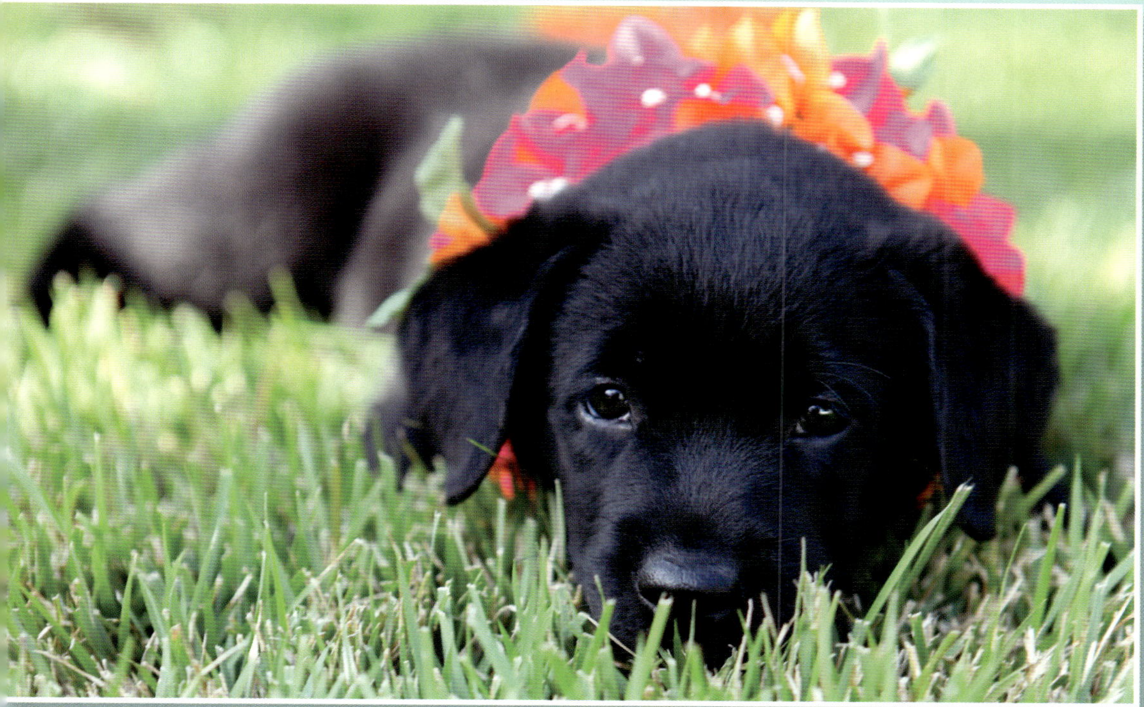

"Being an only puppy has its benefits."

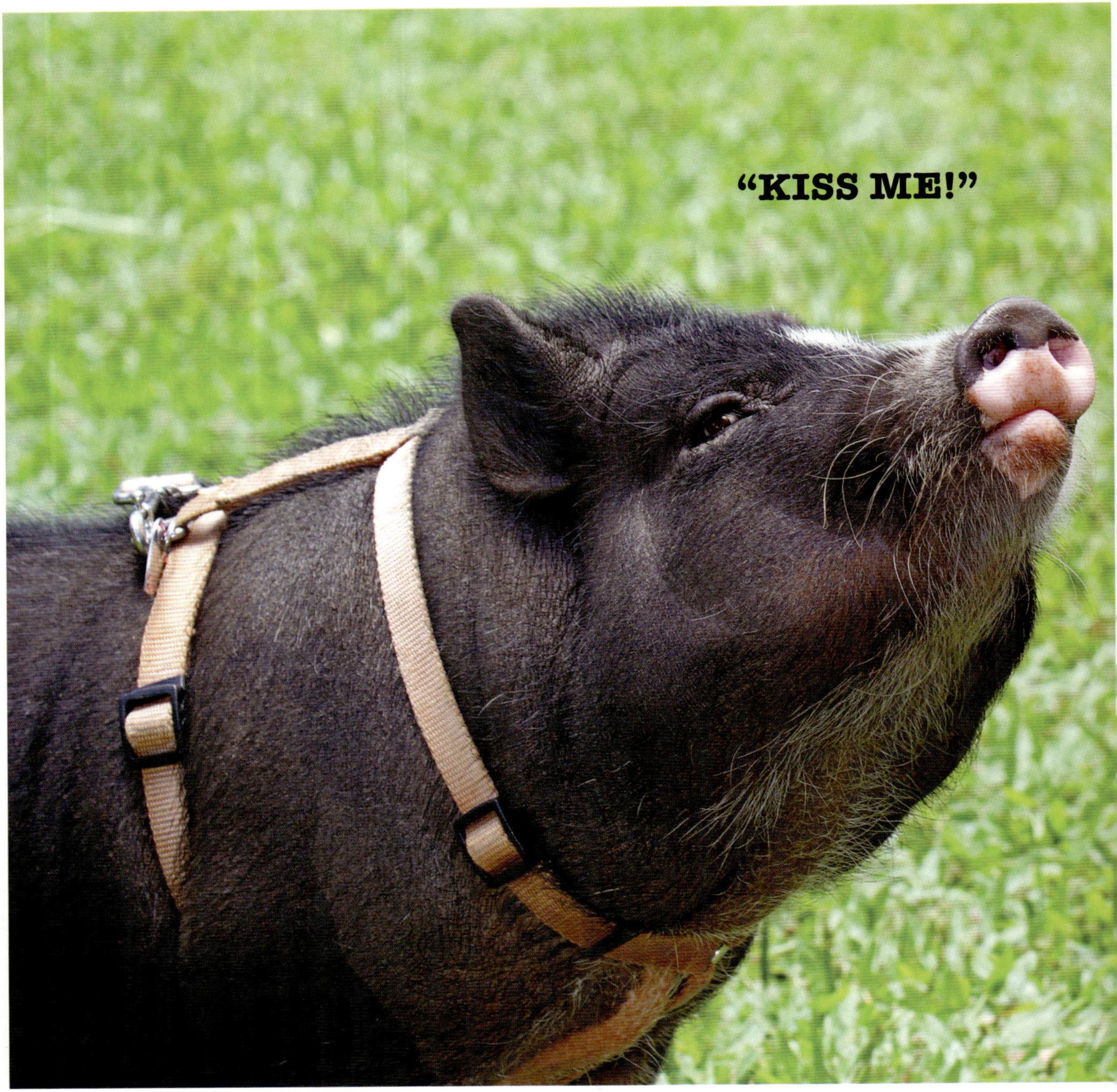
"KISS ME!"

"I smell bacon!
BACON
BACON
BACON!
Oh…
I'm sorry…
I didn't realize
it was you."

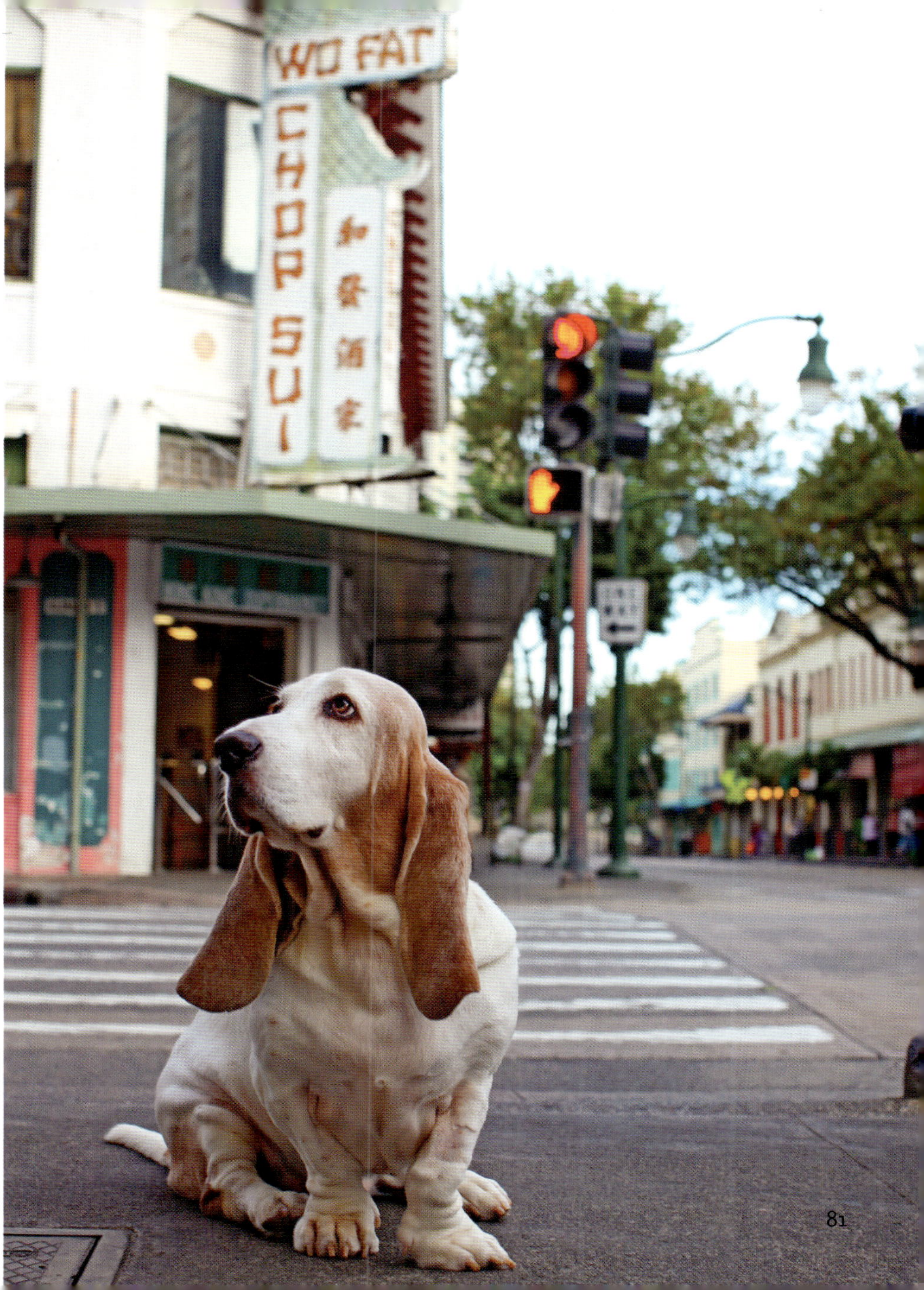

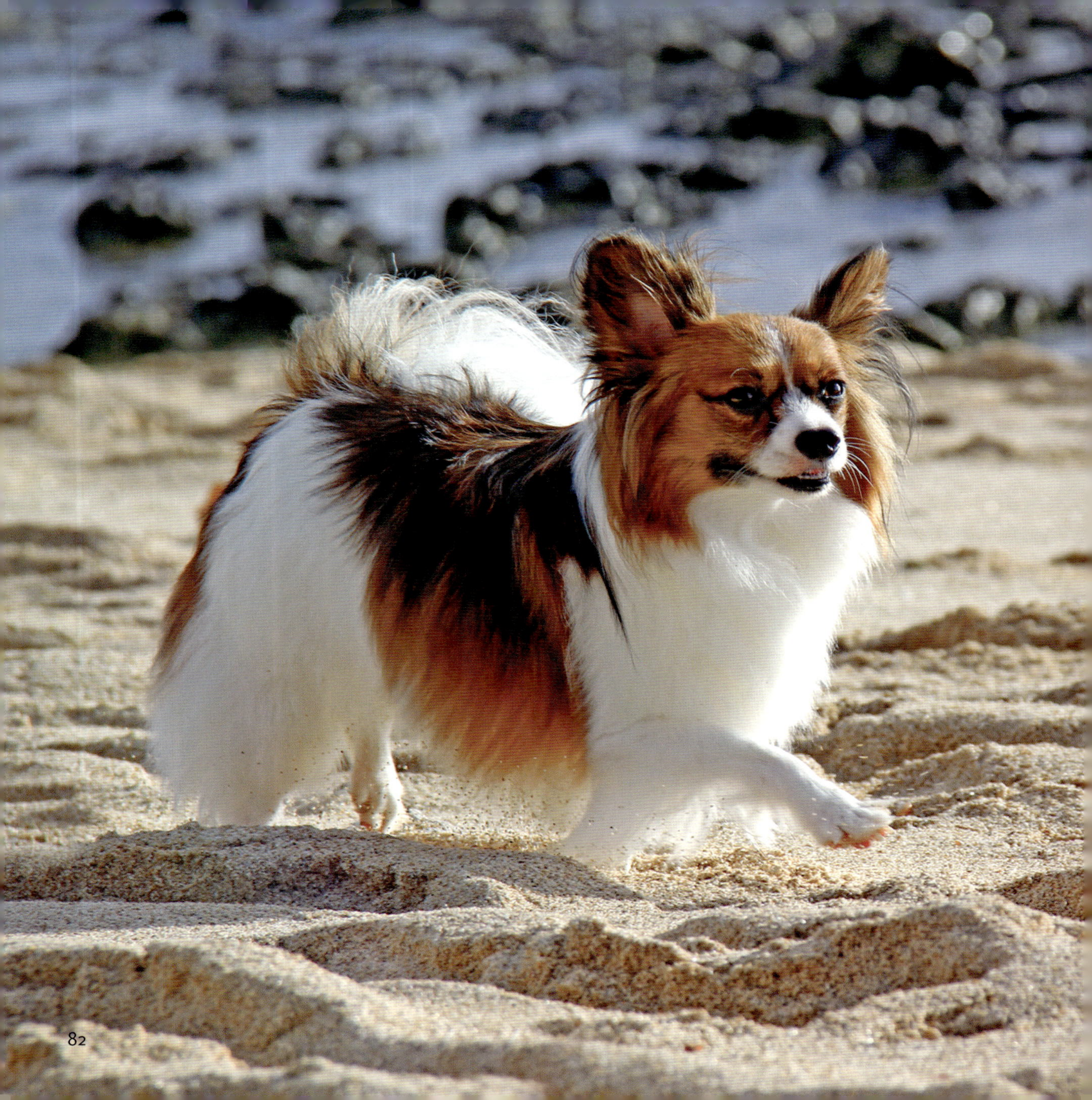

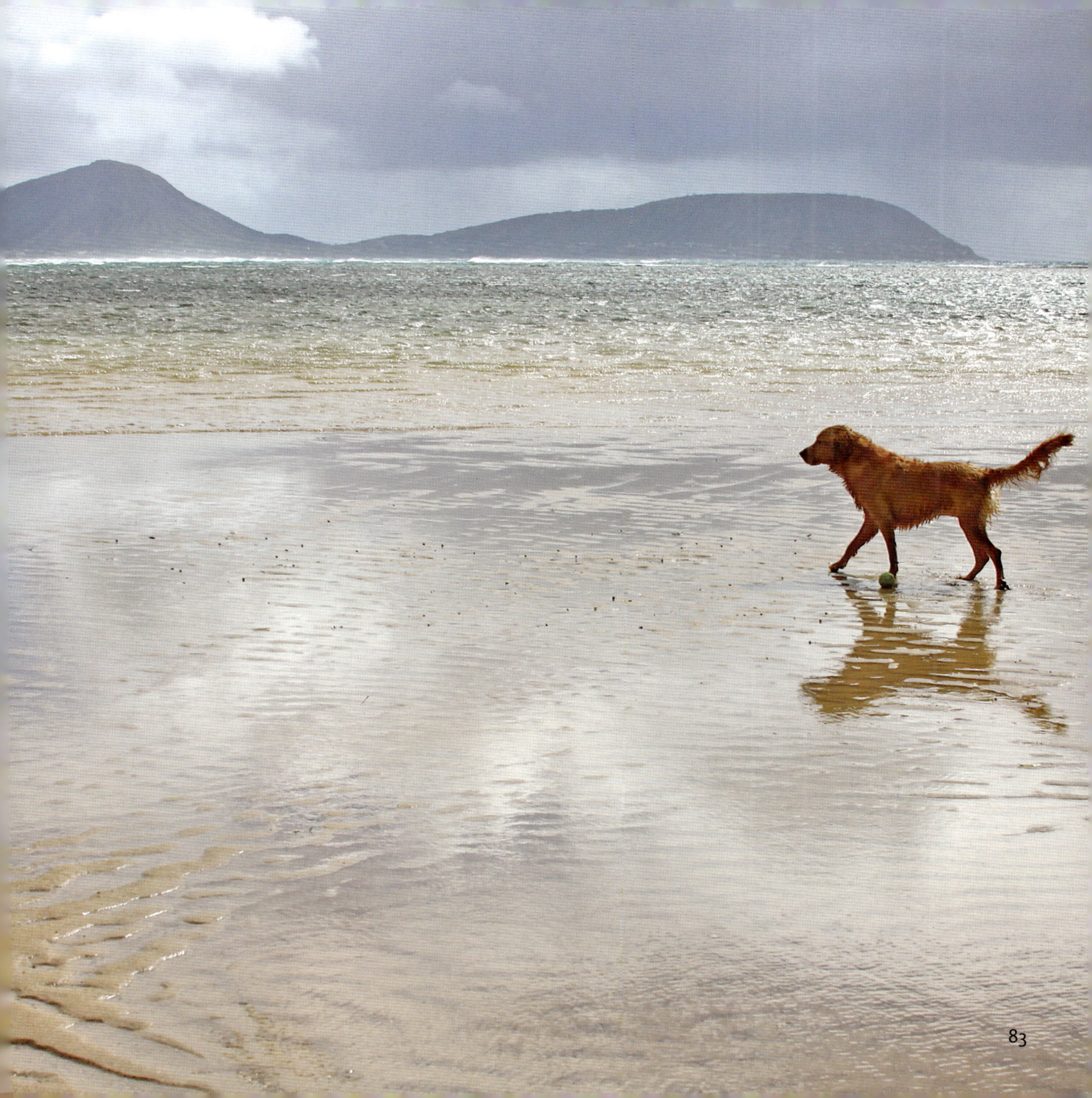

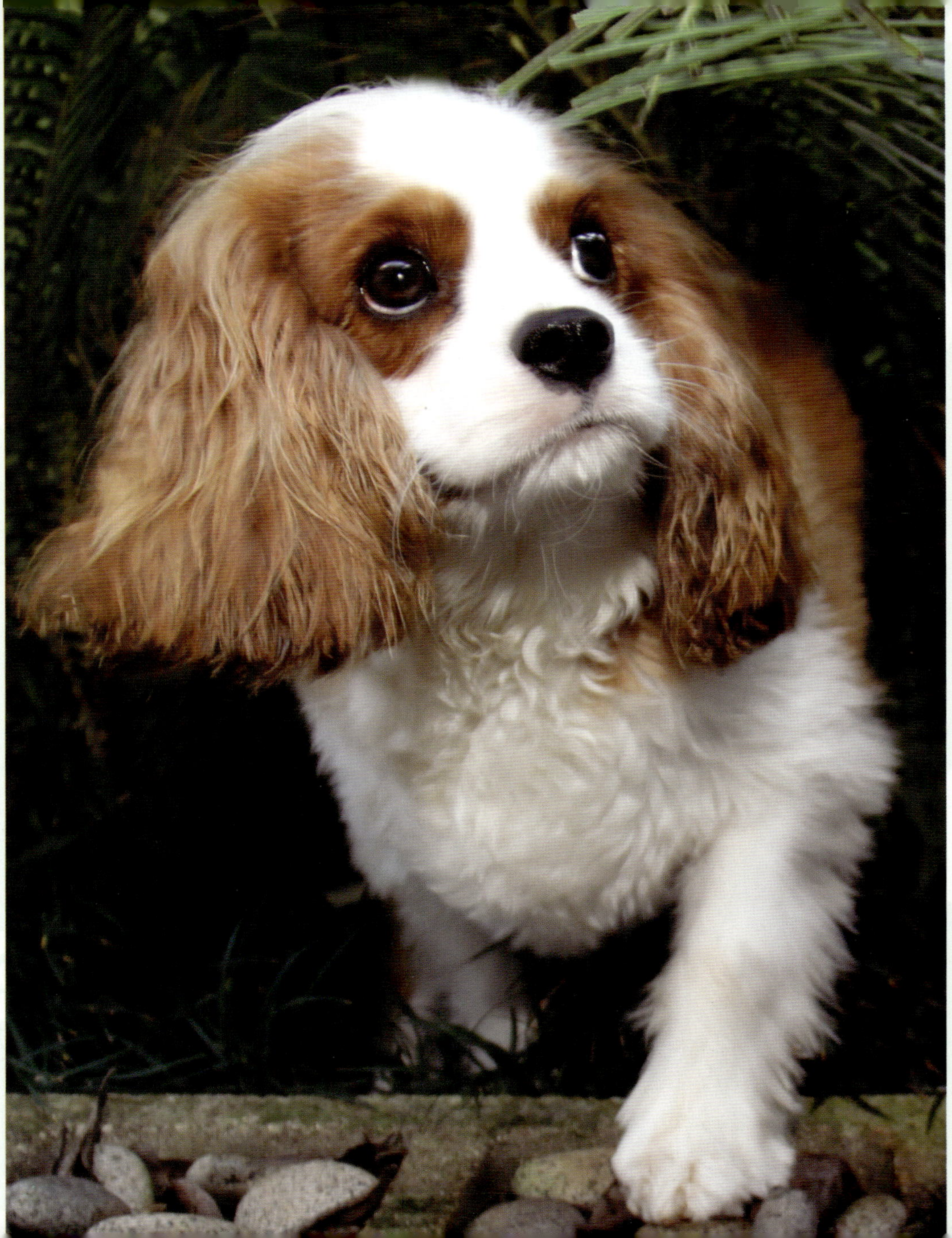

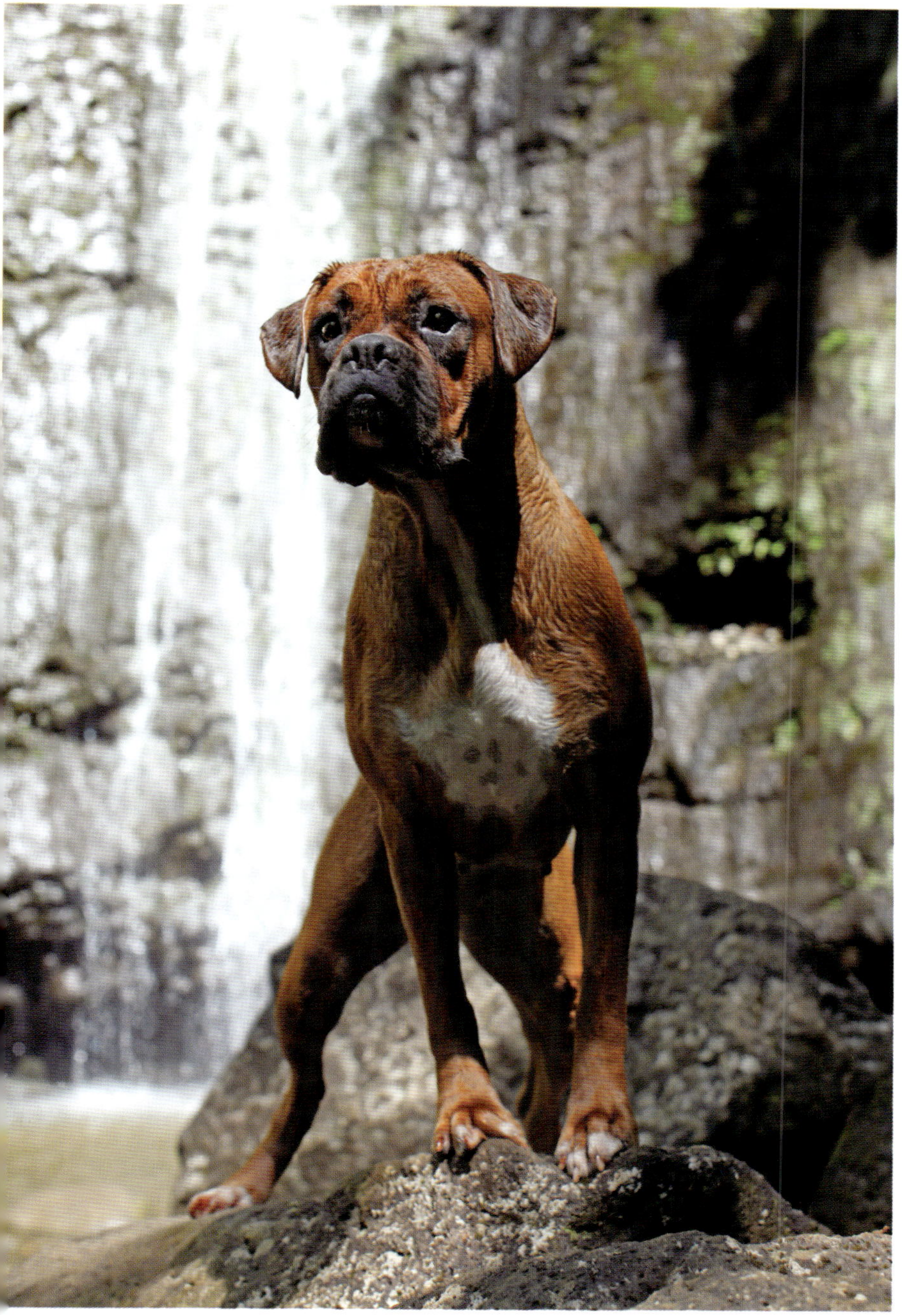

"Could you **HURRY UP** and take the picture? This balancing thing isn't easy."

Tip: Experiment with various angles. In the end, you will have unique and interesting images.

“Meet your total package: fabulous personality and **STUNNING GOOD LOOKS.**”

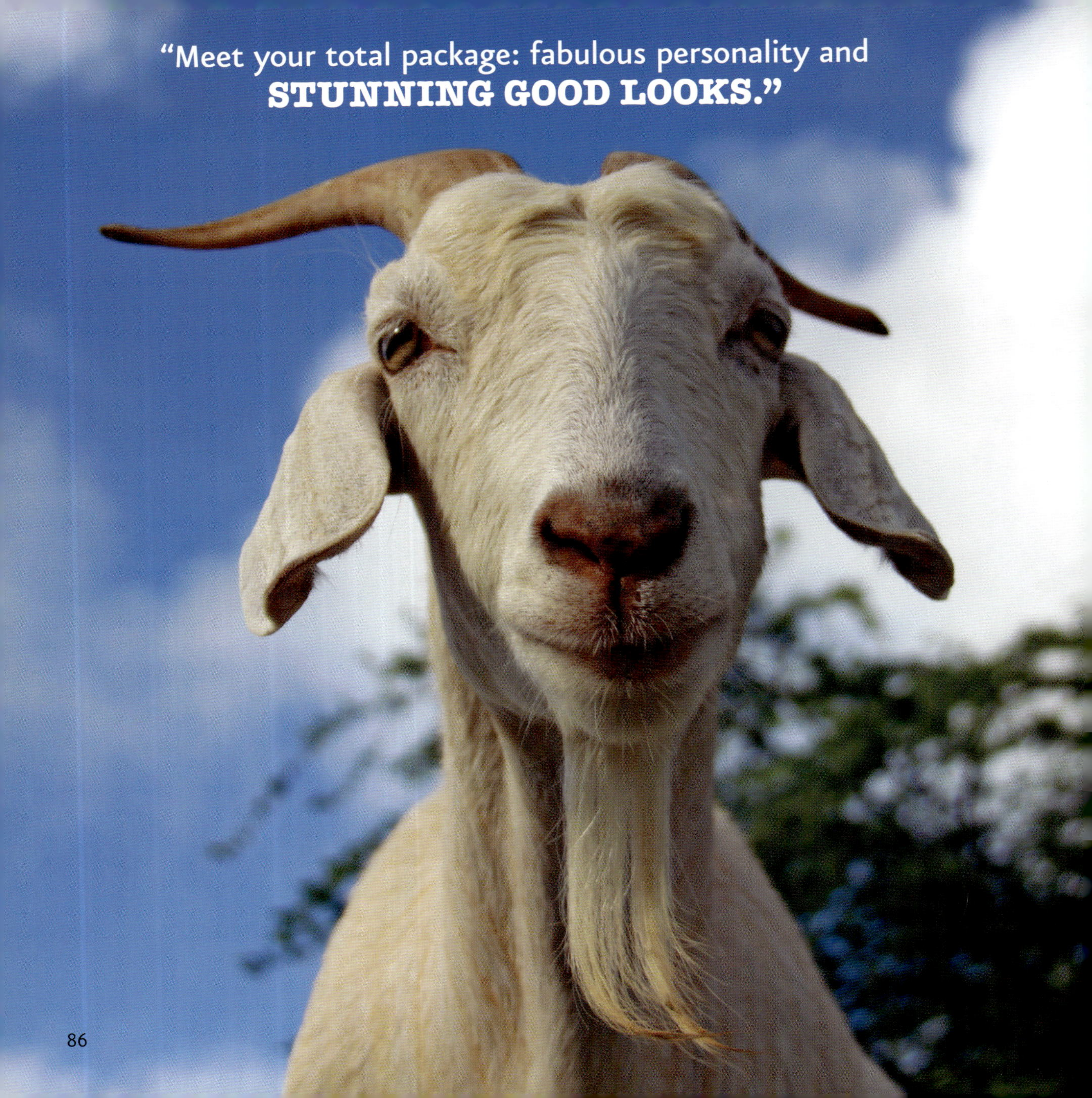

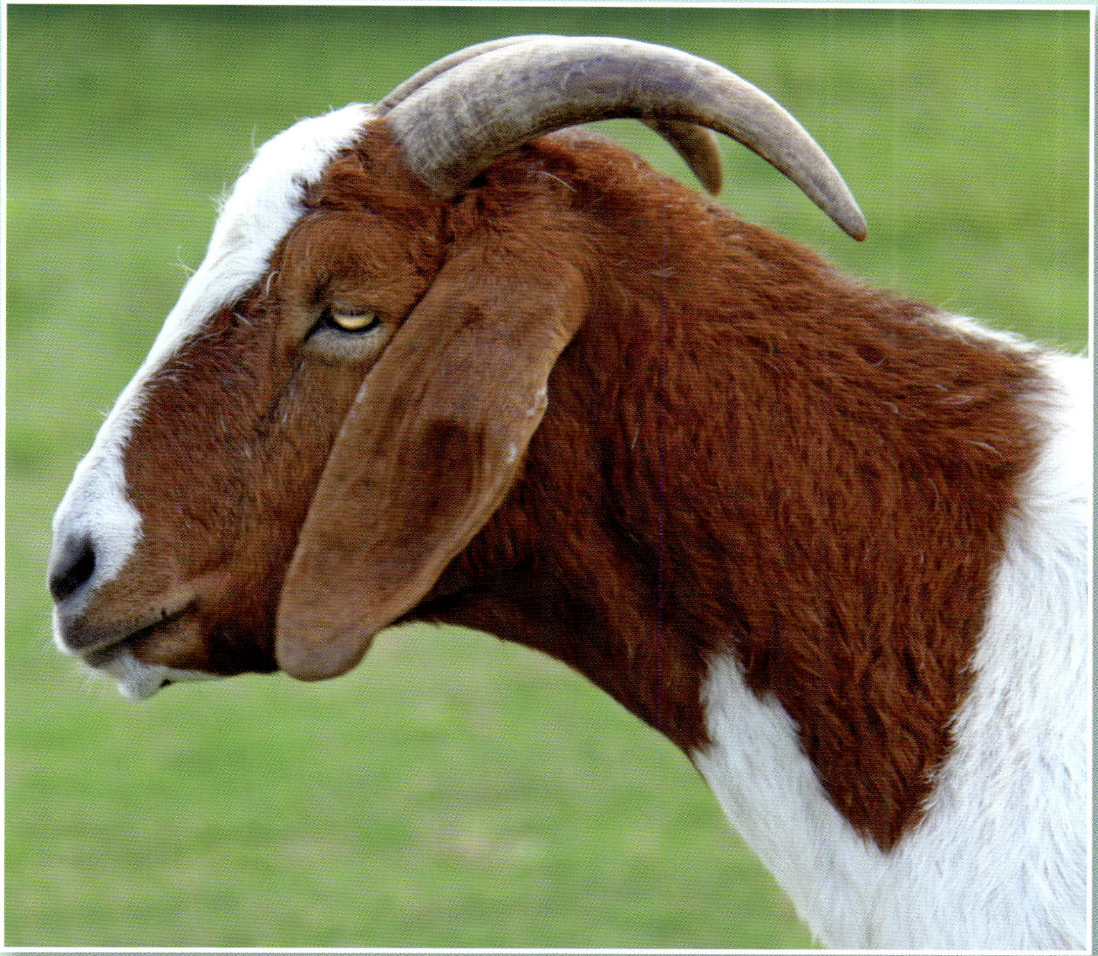

"You've got to be
KIDDING."

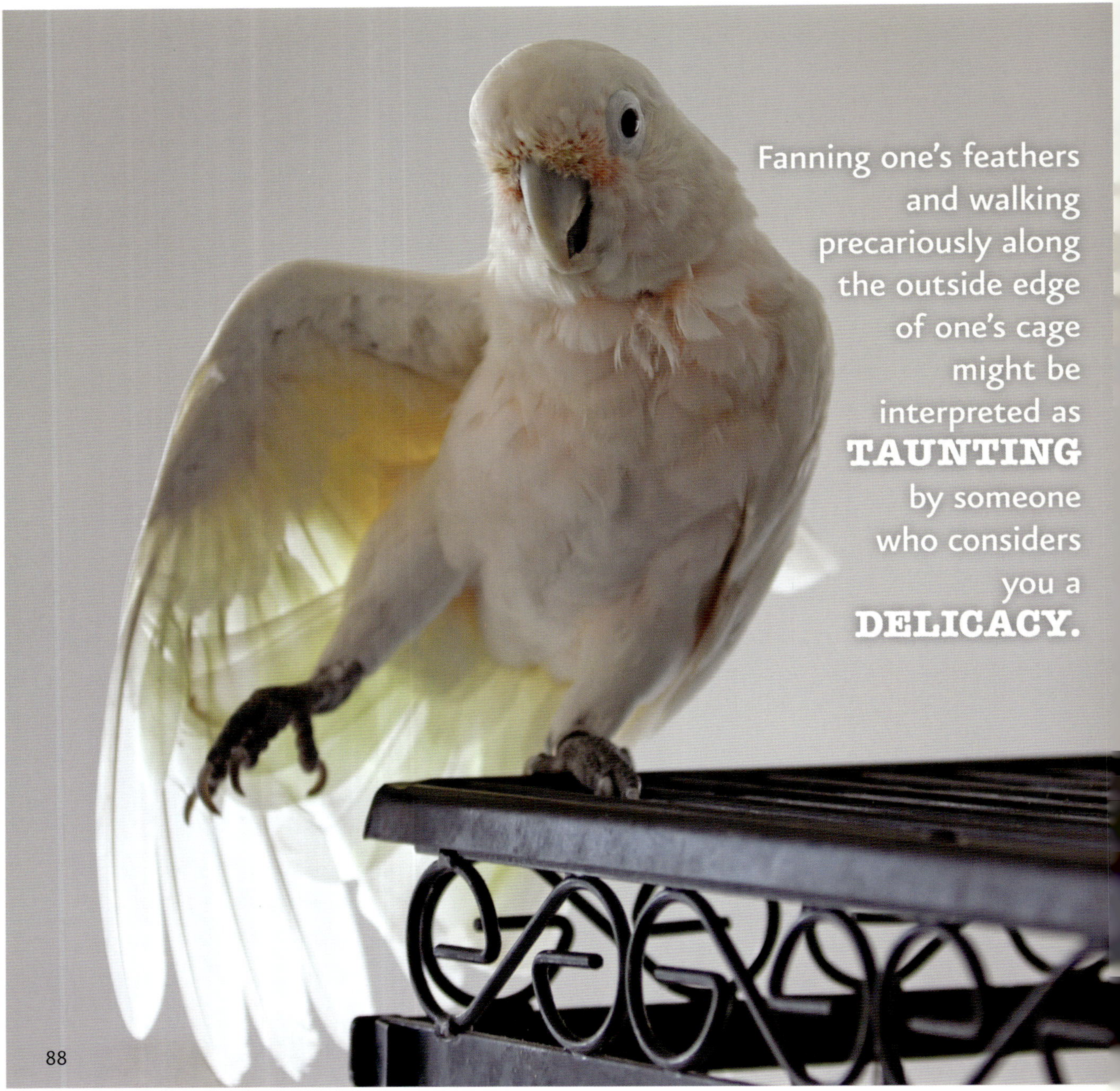

Fanning one's feathers and walking precariously along the outside edge of one's cage might be interpreted as **TAUNTING** by someone who considers you a **DELICACY.**

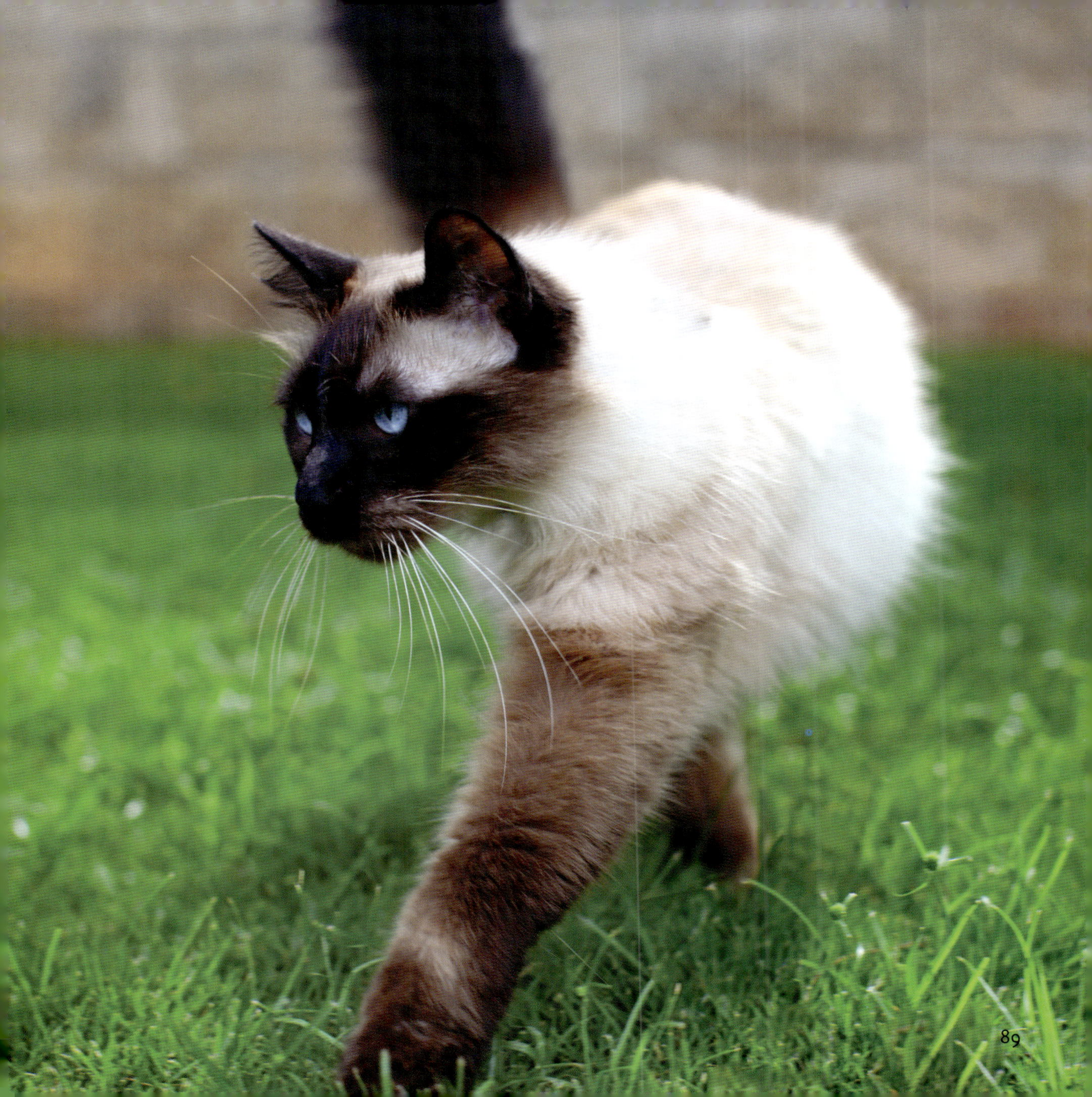

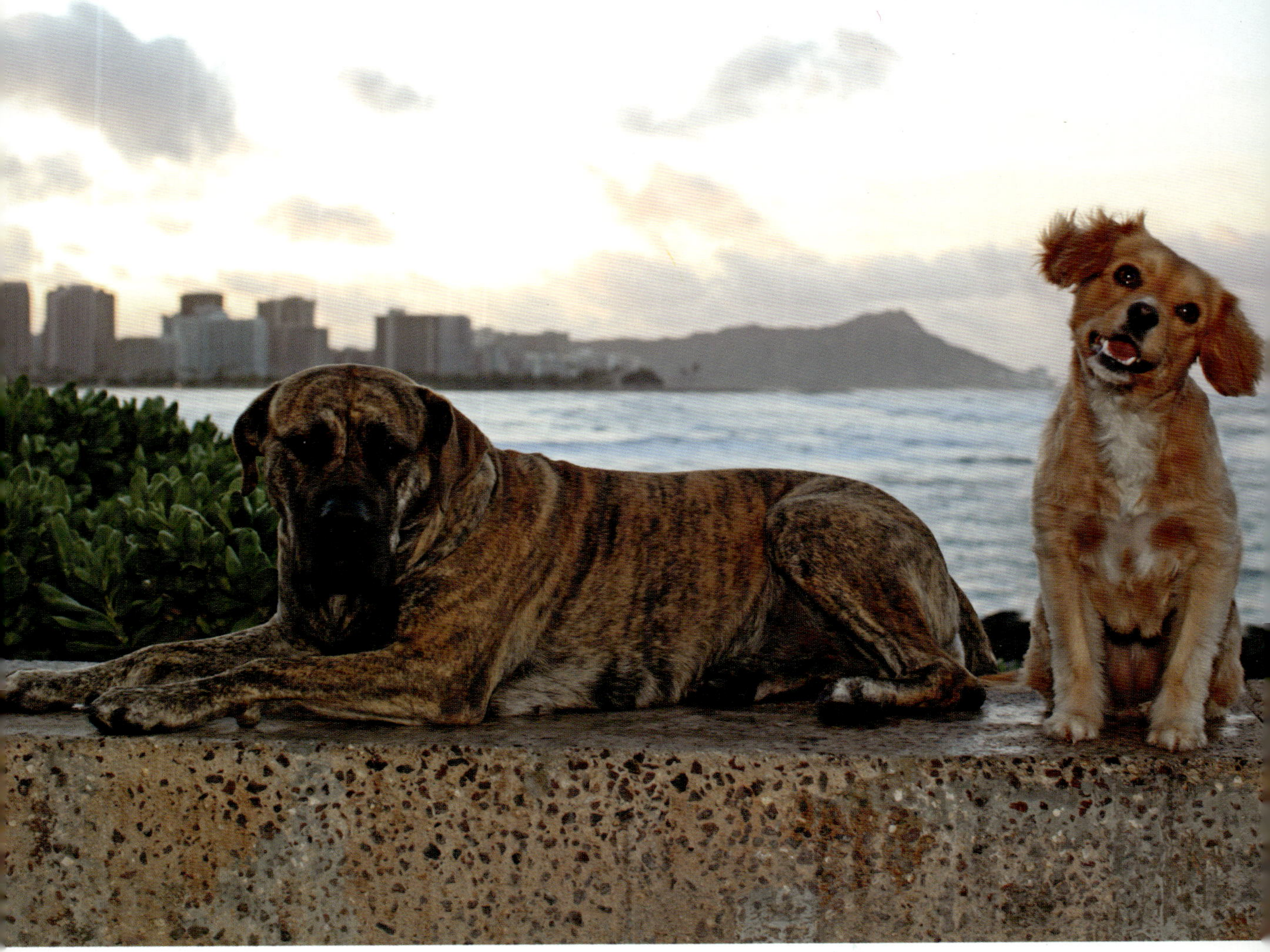

LOL...share the joy.

Tip: When photographing multiple pets, REMEMBER to take some singles, too.

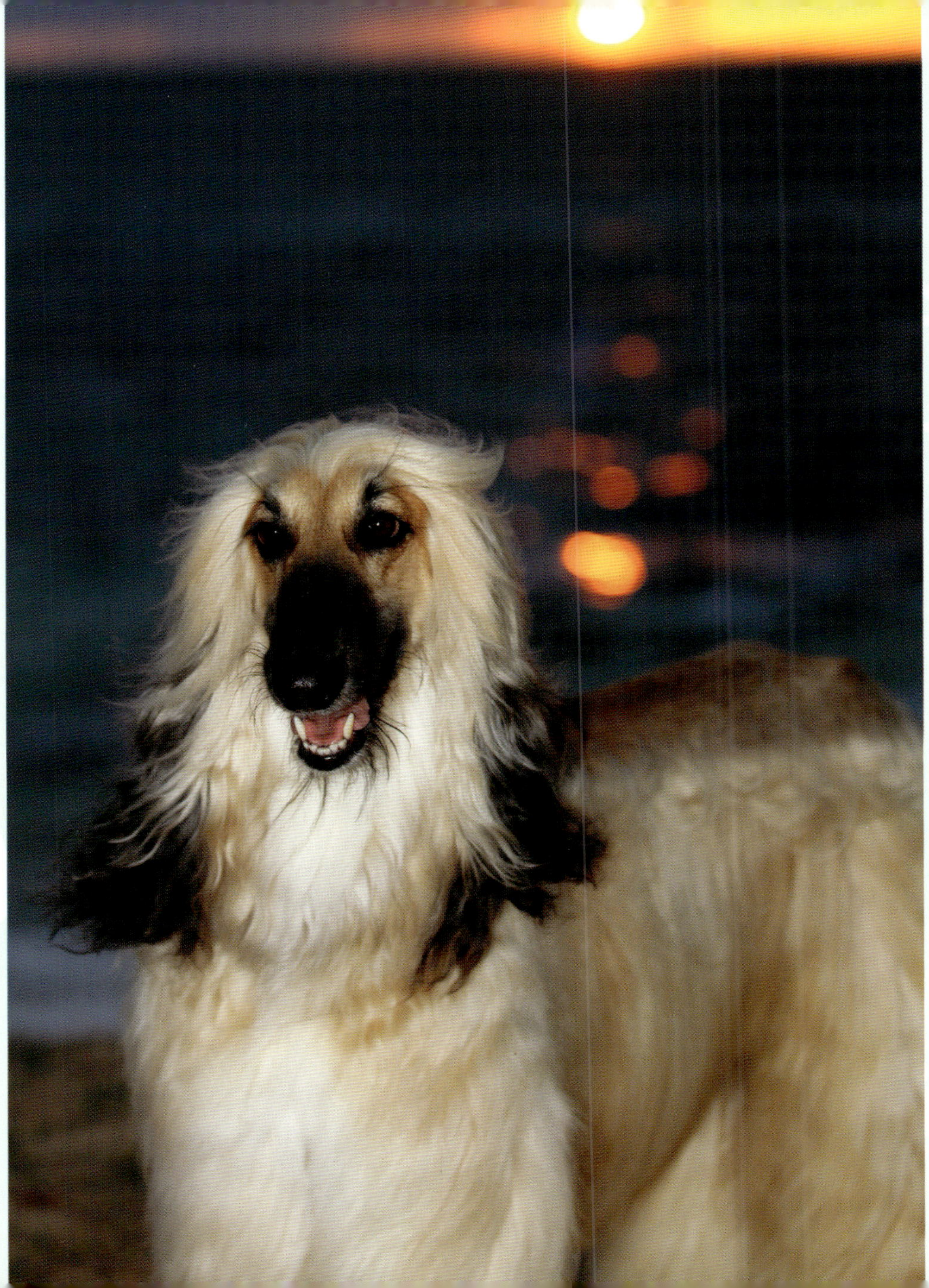

BEST FRIENDS

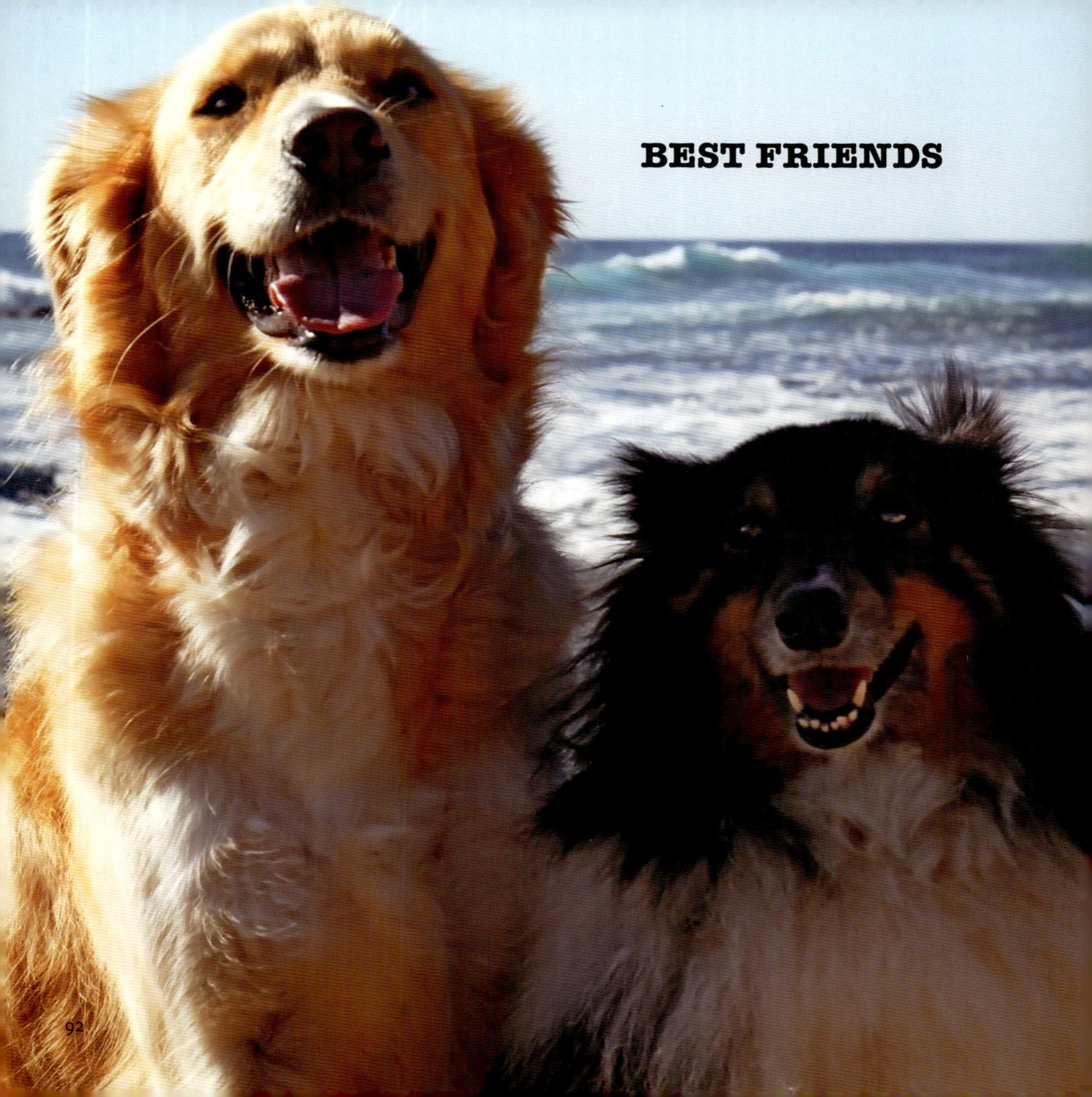

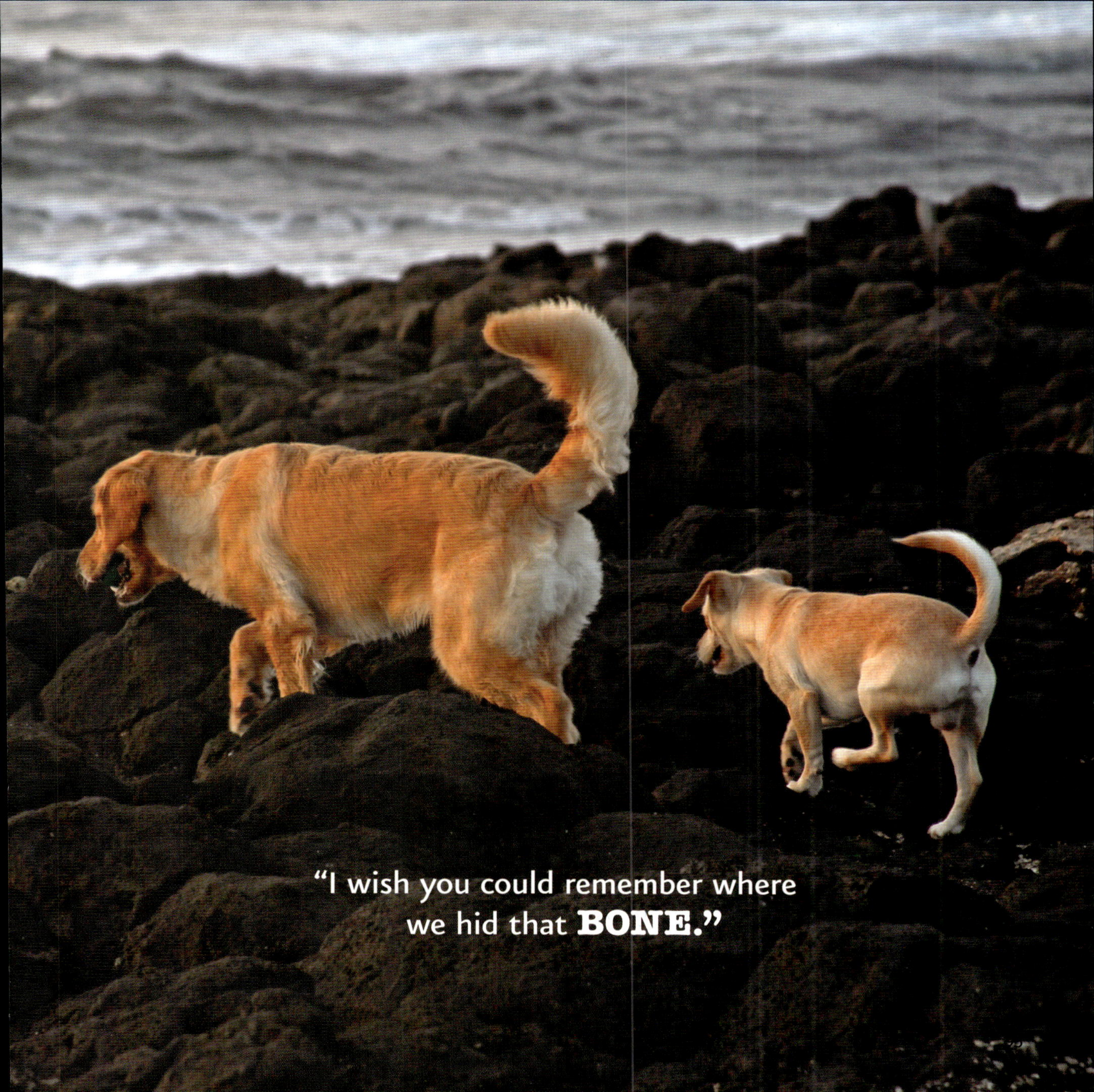

"I wish you could remember where we hid that **BONE.**"

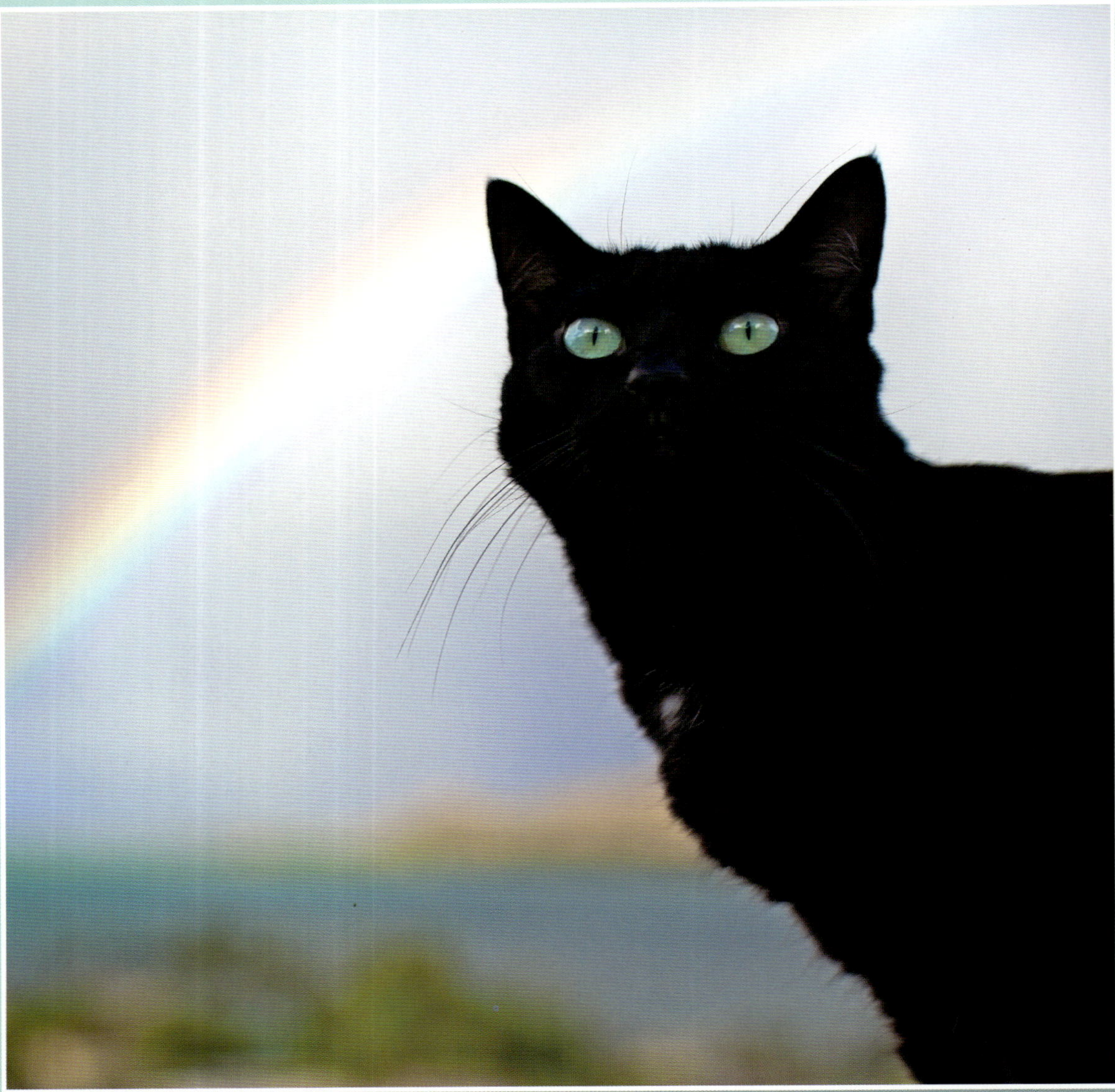

"Birds fly over the rainbow, why then, oh why can't I?
Of course, my intentions would be **HONORABLE.**"

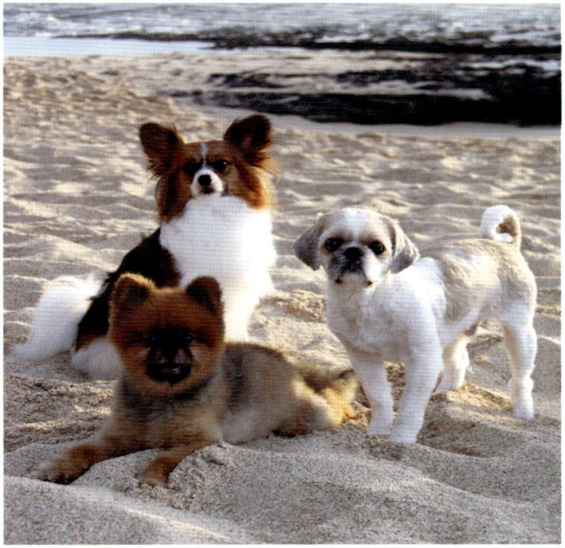

Acknowledgments

A big **MAHALO** to all my furry and feathered models and their pet parents. Indeed, I have been honored to peer through my lens and through their eyes to the depths of their souls. What an incredible gift you all have given me.

Special thanks goes to my #1 "Booth Babe," Auntie Gin Gin (R.I.P), to Sandra Spencer, Dawn Hisaka and to Ron Darby of "The Pet Hui." All have supported my great adventure from the beginning.

Library of Congress Control Number: 2011933058

Visit hawaiianhumane.org to join our animal ʻohana.

ISBN-10: 1-56647-951-7
ISBN-13: 978-1-56647-951-6

Design by Courtney Young

First Printing, August 2011

Mutual Publishing, LLC
1215 Center Street, Suite 210
Honolulu, Hawaiʻi 96816
Ph: 808-732-1709 / Fax: 808-734-4094
email: info@mutualpublishing.com
www.mutualpublishing.com

Printed in Korea

About Deb McGuire

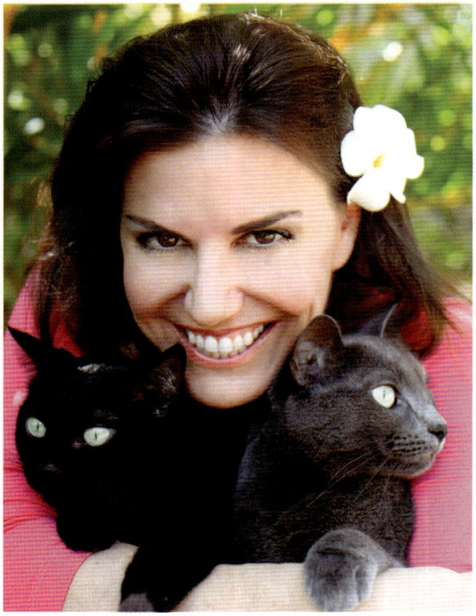

Born and raised in Southern California, Deb McGuire majored in broadcast and print journalism at the University of Southern California. After graduation Deb worked as a reporter, anchor, producer, and radio personality. She was a highly acclaimed celebrity journalist for E! Entertainment Television. Deb has also worked for several major television organizations (including NBC and ABC) and worldwide publications including *People Magazine* and *Fancy Publications*. She has been a commercial model in print and on film, as well as an on-camera spokesperson and actress. Deb still dabbles occasionally in the entertainment field.

Deb and her husband Tim ventured to Hawai'i in 2005. They loved the Islands and decided to stay. The family's other two members, Magic and Sham-rock (both adopted), as well as Deb and her husband chose Hawai'i as their forever home.

In 2009, Deb launched Deb McGuire Pet Photography, also known as Hawai'i Pet Photos, and quickly catapulted to the top of the pet photography industry. In 2010 she was recognized as **"Hawai'i's Favorite Pet Photographer."**